How to Jump-Start Your Husband*

How to Jump-Start Your Husband*

*Wife, Boyfriend, Girlfriend, Mystery Lady, Cute Guy at Work, or That Silver-Haired Devil on the Bus

~Langdon Hill~

Andrews and McMeel, Inc.
A Universal Press Syndicate Company
KANSAS CITY • NEW YORK

Library of Congress Cataloging in Publication Data

Hill, Langdon.
  How to jump-start your husband*.

  1. Love—Anecdotes, facetiae, satire, etc.
2. Love—Miscellanea.   I. Title.
HQ801.H49   1983   646.7'7   83-15153
ISBN 0-8362-7917-4

For Mrs. P and B

Contents

Introduction

"What Exactly Is Jump-Starting? Sounds Kinky, but I'll Bet It Could Be a Lot of Fun"

In the automotive world, jump-starting is using your strong battery to re-energize someone else's weak one. In the world of romance, jump-starting is pretty much the same thing.

It's a fun way to inspire passion in your partner (or in somebody you'd like to be your partner). The trick is to show them that a little "electrifying" stimulation can be good romantic fun.

Who can be a successful jump-starter? Anyone. And you don't have to be a "Total" anything to do it. (When it comes to jump-starting, even a "Partial" woman or man can have a heck of a good time.) In fact, many of the most exciting suggestions in this book come from housewives, office workers, and students—nonprofessional jump-starters just like you.

Where can you jump-start? Most anyplace. From Paris to Pig Oink Falls.

And, what can you jump-start? Most anybody—even someone whose battery has been dead for a *long* time.

Each chapter of this book has step-by-step instructions

1

for a specific jump-starting area (from how to firm up Velveeta-like husbands to how to find someone to jump-start in the first place). Once you've read one chapter, go ahead and check out what the other sex is doing in the next. Remember, almost any suggestion in this book can be used for jump-starting both men *and* women. The only difference is in where you apply the stimulation.

YOUR JUMP-STARTING TOOLBOX

If you've ever tried jump-starting your husband (or wife, boyfriend, girlfriend, mystery lady, cute guy at work, or that silver-haired devil on the bus), you know it takes more than a pair of electrodes and a jar of heavy-duty grease. Jump-starting your loved one (or hoped-to-be loved one) requires caring, affection, and an industrial-sized dose of romance.

It also requires a specialized set of tools. Here's what you'll need:

Jumper Cables. No, you don't need to run down to your local automotive parts store for a pair of copper clamps. Your jumper cable is romance—powered by hundreds of exciting (and shocking) suggestions.

A "Never-Say-Die" Battery. The ultimate power source for passion is *you.* This book will help you to charge up yourself, so that you can electrify almost anyone's battery (Yes, even *his*).

Heavy-Duty Gloves. Jump-starting your husband (etc.) can be a messy business. The key to its success is to treat your loved one with kid gloves. How do you work on his or her engine? Tenderly.

Grease. Before you think this is getting really kinky, the kind of grease I'm talking about is *consistency.* There is no better way to rust up a relationship than to spray it with hot and cold running affection. The suggestions in this book will help you to consistently show your affection—and convince your loved one to show the same in return.

A Good Maintenance Plan. Included in this book is a year-long Jump-Starting Calendar to help keep your relationship running in high gear. With periodic tune-ups, this calendar should help you enjoy a lifetime of revved-up romance.

And a Hammer. If, after doing your best, you find that you're stuck with a lemon, do what all good mechanics do and give your partner a good swift kick in the . . . romance. And, if even that doesn't work, remember that you can frequently get a good deal on a trade-in.

1

"My Marriage Is about as Passionate as Velveeta Cheese. How Can I Jump-Start My Husband?"

Before we get to the nitty-gritty of jump-starting, you should first be aware that each and every jump-starter has a number of rights in a relationship.

Step One in jump-starting your husband is knowing your Romantic Warranty of Rights:

1) *You have the right to feel loved—at all times.* If your romantic partner is full of love and adoration one moment, but has all the warmth of a Siberian porcupine the next, set him straight—now.

2) *You have the right to have time alone with your partner.* What does your television have that you don't have? If the answer is, "My husband," tell him to put some electricity back into your relationship or face being unplugged.

3) *You have the right to say, "This is what I want."* Let your partner know what you want in clear and precise terms. A little shock to his system might be just what is needed.

4) *You have the right to physical closeness.* And you have the right to this closeness *without* sex as a requirement.

5) *You have the right to excitement.* Since when did you

promise to love, honor, and be bored to tears?

6) *You have the right to be pampered—and to pamper.*
(And we're not talking about diapers here.) If your husband
says he's "too much of a real man" for this—hit him in the
face with a quiche.

7) *You have the right to be seriously less-than-perfect.*
As one wise person wrote: "I'm an absolutely perfect person, except when I'm making a mistake."

8) *You have the right to expect courtesy at all times.* The
days of *gentle*men and ladies are not behind us. How do you
tell if he's a gentleman? A gentleman gives you flowers—a
Neanderthal eats them.

9) *You have the right to moral support from your partner.*
The most successful romantic partners are also best friends.
(Who else can you turn to when the toilet plugs up for the
forty-seventh time?)

10) *And you have the right to dream.* Before you can take
your relationship to its limits, you have to know where you
want it to go.

Step Two in jump-starting your husband is preparing a
consistent plan of romantic attack. By consistently showing
him that a little passionate romance can be fun, you should be
able to jump-start his own romantic engine. Even Velveeta-
like hubbies should firm up into world-class romantics when
faced with the following Thirty-Day Jump-Starting Plan:

Day One. Tell your loved one "I love you" when he
least expects it.

Day Two. Blow up your television (or just unplug it) and
take a walk together this evening.

Day Three. Look up the meanings of the words, "hug,"
"cuddle," and "snuggle" in the dictionary and then follow
directions.

Day Four. Catch a fun late-night movie at home (like

Abbott and Costello Meet Brooke Shields or *I Was a Teenage Stockbroker*). Be sure to pop up several tons of popcorn. Who knows when the U.S. Marine Corps might drop by?

Day Five. Surprise your spouse with an intimate candlelit dinner at home. If you have children, set up a fun dinner for them in a secluded spot—like at a friend's house in Paraguay. (More on parents and romance later.)

Day Six. Take your husband out on a date, but don't tell him what you're going to do ahead of time. Don't worry—it will be good for him, too.

Day Seven. Go bicycling or jogging together. And if the thought of sweating in the great outdoors bothers you, you can always try a little indoor aerobic cuddling.

Day Eight. Hold a picnic in your backyard or living room. And, if you're worried about missing out on nature—don't. Biologists have clearly shown that you don't have to leave home to discover wildlife.

Day Nine. Catch a movie (at a drive-in, if possible). You're sure to find more to nibble on than just Reese's Pieces.

Day Ten. Test drive a Mercedes tonight. To get the full effect, take a spin (or two) through your very own neighborhood. Now, don't be a snob. Make sure you wave and smile at the Joneses next door. (By the way, no purchase is required.)

Day Eleven. Experience the joys of a sensual massage at bedtime. (Don't let him be piggy—show him that he kneads you, too.) Try to keep it to just "massaging" tonight.

Day Twelve. Re-experience the joys of kissing this evening. Sit across from each other and, without using your hands, just kiss. While extracurricular touching is semistrictly discouraged, where you kiss each other is up to you.

Day Thirteen. Spend the night alone together. No television. No children. No interruptions.

Day Fourteen. Have breakfast, lunch, and/or dinner in bed today. Don't forget about dessert.

Day Fifteen. Flex your maturity and have a pillow fight tonight. Formal wear is not required.

Day Sixteen. Surprise your husband with flowers today. And, yes, men like to get flowers, too. (More on this later.)

Day Seventeen. Mail your loved one a love letter. Feel free to be very creative. (If you're particularly absent-minded, make absolutely sure to get the address right. Aunt Mathilda would not be amused.)

Day Eighteen. Telephone your husband at work today. Be daring. You'll be amazed what happens when you reach out and really touch someone.

Day Nineteen. Make tonight's meal Mexican and "chimichanga" the night away. (Look it up—I dare you.)

Day Twenty. Make a list entitled, "This is why I love you," and give it to your loved one. If you're stuck for poetic-sounding reasons, take your paper and pen, go down to your nearest greeting card shop, and copy a few dozen of theirs.

Day Twenty-One. Make tonight's meal French and experience the food of romance. Believe me, the only phrase you'll need is "Voulez-vous cuddle, etc.?"

Day Twenty-Two. Get dressed in your finest and escape to an intimate restaurant. If you're low on bucks, just order dessert and coffee. By "hurrying," you might get out in under two hours or so.

Day Twenty-Three. Try a little classy Italian food tonight. Buy a bottle of fine red wine and send out for pizza.

Day Twenty-Four. Take a drive in your car and re-experience the joys of necking. As all adolescents know, this is one way to really put yourself in touch with your hormones.

Day Twenty-Five. Enjoy a Japanese meal "Geisha" style in your living room. If you feel really daring, grab your sushi and head for a candlelit bubble bath. (This is especially stimulating for those of you who have considered pearl diving as a career.)

Day Twenty-Six. Make a list entitled, "I like it when you do this," and give it to your husband.

Day Twenty-Seven. Make a list entitled, "I would like to try this," and give it to your husband.

Day Twenty-Eight. Pamper your husband into submission tonight. (Have you ever seen a grown man cry "Yes!"?)

Day Twenty-Nine. Re-exchange your romantic vows today.

Day Thirty. And, together, make a new Thirty-Day Plan for Romance.

This Thirty-Day Plan is a great way to add a lot of zip to your overall relationship. But, what do you do when the zip's been zapped in a specific romantic area? If this has happened to you, it's time for a little "spot" jump-starting.

Here are a number of intriguing questions (many of which were actually submitted by readers of "Romance!," my nationally syndicated newspaper column) and their romantic answers.

Q. I am a twenty-four-year-old woman, happily married for over three years to the most wonderful man in the world. However, I do have a problem: The only place my husband will make love to me is in the back of his pickup truck. (It is where we first made love and he thinks it's the most romantic place in the world.)

It's pretty rough to be dragged out of bed in the middle of

the night to "enjoy a romantic interlude under the stars." Besides, the neighbors' family room overlooks our driveway. It's bad enough in warm weather, but now it's getting cold, and last winter I had the sniffles for months. What can I do?—"Bored Stiff"

A. I've heard of getting picked up before, but getting "pickupped" is a new one on me. While your husband may be a wonderful man otherwise, his idea of a "romantic evening" is more than slightly out of gear. In fact, if he (and you) keep trucking, your marriage stands a good chance of going flat.

But, Chevy lovers, take heart. Romantic help is on the way. Try this plan of attack:

Step One: Learn how to say, "This is want I *want.*" A marriage is an equal partnership. You have just as much to say about your romantic interludes as your husband.

If he continually suggests something you don't want to do, tell him lovingly, "Thank you, darling, but this is what I want." Then grab him and show him exactly what you mean.

Step Two: A little jump-starting "shock therapy" has been known to work wonders. Here are just two real-life romance stories to help you get out of the driveway.

—The Great Hotel Getaway. On a Friday afternoon, Barbara called her husband and asked him to meet her at a swank hotel bar for drinks after work. After their second round, Barbara smiled, dropped a room key into her husband's hand, and told him to meet her there in fifteen minutes. He did. They left the hotel, still smiling two days later.

—Kidnapped Campers. Jennifer took her husband out for what was supposed to be a Saturday morning brunch. When she stopped driving the car, after two hours, they had arrived at a beautiful mountain camping area. In their truck Jennifer

10

had stowed food, a tent, gear, and two seriously cuddly sleeping bags (the kind that zip together). Though it got below freezing that evening, she said that they "didn't have a chance to notice."

When camping, romantics should be very aware of hypothermia—a condition in which your body temperature lowers to life-threatening levels. (Check with your local Red Cross for details.) Experts tell me that one of the best ways to combat hypothermia is to take off your cold clothes and snuggle together in your sleeping bag for warmth. Campers (and non-campers) would be well advised to practice this before, during, and after their trip.

And for those of you whose idea of a strenuous hike is getting from the couch to the bathroom at halftime, try pitching your pup tent in your bedroom.

Step Three: If, after all this, you're still seeing the U.S.A. from your Chevrolet, take out a loan and buy yourself a camper.

Some husbands are so unromantic that only teamwork can help. "Ready for the Glue Factory" found this out when she wrote:

Q. I've got a problem. I love romance, but my husband is as romantic as a Clydesdale. What can I do?

A. Outside of putting him out to stud, one of the most effective ways to deal with this problem is to use the Romantic Buddy System. Here's how it works:

First, you find a friend who is willing to help you concoct a passionate surprise for your hubby—in exchange for the same help later on. (This is a lot easier to do than it may seem. Trust me.)

Next, you—with your sneaky friend providing all the romantic "magic"—put together an evening that is best explained by Thelma in the following romance novelette:

It was a dark and homey night. My passion, my love, my husband, my Ralph languidly stretched across the sofa—his blue eyes intently scanning the television. I felt my heart leap with unbridled desire when he seductively scratched his groin while opening another Budweiser. What a man. What an evening.

Little did he know, however, that this was to be no ordinary night.

"Ralph," I called. My entire being flushed with fire when he burped in response. "We need to go to the store for some dog food."

"What do you want me to do?" he replied. "Alert the media?"

"No," I whispered. "I want you to get your bod off that couch and come with me or I'll cancel your subscription to *Cosmopolitan.* "

An instant later, he followed me out the door.

"But, Thelma. We don't have a dog," said Ralph.

"I know," I smiled.

After a thrilling forty-five-minute tour of the neighborhood, we returned home. The trap was set. My coconspirator had come, done her work, and gone.

Ralph opened the front door and found a trail of elegant roses (borrowed from a neighbor's bush) leading from the door to the dining room. Waiting in the dining room was an intimate candlelit dinner of Boeuf à la Thelma (burgers and sautéed mushrooms) and a jug of chilled wine—with a sensible screw top.

After dinner, I motioned toward another trail of flowers leading back to a candlelit bubble bath and asked him if he was ready for dessert. He was.

The bathtub was filled with steaming foam. A chilled

bottle of champagne was nestled in a bucket by its side. On the way in, Ralph saw that yet another trail of flowers led back to the bedroom.

"I think I feel something in my loins," he breathed as he slipped his ample body into the bubble-filled pit of passion.

"You do," I nodded. "You do."

Romance is definitely a two-way street. While these suggestions are aimed at wives (hints for husbands are in the next chapter), their purpose is to get reluctant husbands to wake up and add their share of romance to relationships.

Recent studies have shown that men and women are much more alike when it comes to romance than we think. Each sex needs and appreciates tenderness. Everyone wants and desires love. One of the best known ways to show someone that you care is to send flowers. But, the question that remains is . . .

Q. Is it okay for a woman to send a man flowers? I think it works both ways, but I'm not sure. Can you help?— "Don't Want to Make a Ms.-take"

A. Yes, a thousand buds, yes. It's not only okay to send a man flowers, in many cases it's vital. Flowers, for both sexes, are one of the most obvious symbols of affection. And for many men, the more obvious you are, the better.

The key word to keep in mind when selecting flowers for a man is "price." This isn't unromantic, it's just good, common sense. Why buy your loved one a megabuck arrangement when you could get a used Volkswagen instead?

Seriously, don't be afraid to buy just one flower for your husband. It doesn't mean you're cheap. It means you're smart. In fact, in the traditional language of flowers, a single flower frequently carries more meaning than a truckload.

Here are the meanings of a *single* flower from a number of common, and not so common, floral varieties.

Camellia (red)—You're a flame in my heart.

Camellia (white)—You're adorable.

Carnation (pink)—I'll never forget you.

Carnation (solid color)—Yes, a thousand times, yes.

Carnation (white)—Pure love.

Chrysanthemum (red)—I love you.

Chrysanthemum (white)—Truth.

Daffodil—The sun is always shining when I'm with you.

Daisy—Loyal love.

Fern—You are magic.

Forget-me-not—True love.

Gardenia—Secret love.

Gladiola—I'm really sincere.

Gloxinia—Love at first sight.

Lily (white)—It's heavenly to be with you.

Orange blossom—Eternal love.

Orchid—You're beautiful.

Primrose—I can't live without you.

Rose (hibiscus)—Delicate beauty.

Rose (pink)—Perfect happiness.

Rose (red)—I love you.

Rose (thornless)—Love at first sight.

Rose (white)—You are heavenly.

Rosebud—Beauty and youth.

Tulip—Perfect lover.

Violet (white)—Let's take a chance at happiness.

And, if you're looking for something a little more obscure, try:

Cactus—The symbol of endurance.

Garlic—For courage and strength.

Nasturtium—For conquest.

Or a Dried White Rose—which means, "Death is preferable to loss of virtue." Honestly.

Now that you have that one special flower, don't just shove it under your hubby's nose. Take some time to contemplate the perfect delivery. Some suggestions:

—Gift-wrap it and hide your package in an unusual location—on his pillow, in the refrigerator, in the shower, in his underwear drawer (this is definitely not recommended for cactus), or on the front seat of his car.

—Arrange for your waiter or waitress to present it during an elegant dinner. It's amazing what a tiny tip will do.

—If you walk or jog together, hide your surprise in a convenient bush or tree ahead of time and then pull it out at the appropriate moment. (Wait until the neighbors see this.)

—Follow him to the grocery store (yes, some husbands actually do the shopping) and drop the flower into his basket when he's not looking.

—Arrange to have a friend deliver it to him at work. (That should arouse his corporate spirit.)

—Or hide it in the dishwasher and then ask him to do the dishes. (See what a little romance can get you?)

What if you'd like to go *further* than flowers? What if you're wondering . . .

Q. Is it okay for a woman to take charge of a romance?

A. Of course it is. In many relationships a frontal assault is just what is needed.

Here are just four real-life examples of romantic women who have taken charge and won.

—"On our third wedding anniversary," wrote Karen, "I sent my husband out on an errand and lit some candles, poured some wine, and then greeted him at the door fully dressed in my wedding gown, veil, and even the garter. I thought he was going to cry. It was the most romantic moment of our marriage.''

—Terry took musical charge of her romance. "This year I wanted to let my groom of three months know what a special song he puts in my heart. We both enjoy music and I wanted him to enjoy his birthday listening to his favorite songs, 'live.' For a small donation, I hired the nearby high school marching band to come to his office and play his favorite songs. He was quite surprised to open the office door to one hundred or so marching musicians. The flag and cheer lines came also and added extra excitement.''

—Lorette may not be subtle, but she gets results. "After being divorced for seven and a half years, I met my superspecial man in church,'' she wrote. "I was frightened to care for someone again, but I decided to try. To show him how I cared, I'd leave him little notes, such as the one I left in the refrigerator with a picture of a tomato in it that said, 'I'll be your tomato anytime,' and one with a picture of Caress soap that said, 'If you want extra caressing, just ask.' The best part is that he saves every one of them.''

—And Mrs. Edward C. went straight to the source with her noteworthy suggestion. "Place your romantic note in your lover's shorts while they're in the bureau drawer. Imagine the fun if he gets to the office before hearing the 'crackle, crackle' of the paper.''

Some women make a plan, check it twice, get ready to be naughty (and nice), but then have second thoughts. You know the ones—"How can I be sexy when I look like Cellulite City?'' or "I look just like Raquel Welch—at age six.'' What they're really asking is . . .

Q. What makes a woman sexy?

A. This may surprise you, but the answer isn't herbal shampoo and tight-fitting jeans. A few of the characteristics that I find sexy in a woman are:

—A spirit of adventure. Did you know that there are some women out there who can have more fun with their husbands in the frozen food section of the supermarket than most others can have in a hot tub with Tom Selleck?

Well, maybe not. But it is true that some women can find fun and adventure in almost everything they do—and this includes romance.

—A sense of humor. I'm willing to grant that seriousness is important—on occasion—but few things are as attractive as a good sense of humor. How else could you live through moments like tripping while putting on your underwear in the morning, stumbling while walking to your table in a restaurant, or grabbing for your lover in bed and nearly knocking him out in the process?

—Independence. Don't be fooled by the macho man's "back to basics approach to sexiness": "You, the woman, do all the work and I, basically, get to do just about anything I damn well please." Gag me with a gold medallion.

A sexy woman knows what she wants and isn't afraid to work to get it.

—Intensity. Life is too short to be a Norma (or Norman) Neutral. You can't expect to start a passionate fire if you don't give off a few sparks first.

—Intelligence. When someone loves you, he doesn't care if you know the name of the capital of Tibet or how many square roots it takes to make a pi. What he is looking for is a partner with a firm, common-sense understanding of the world around her.

—Caring. How can you tell if a woman is caring? I look for signs of this in how she handles children, pets, and

17

klutzes. All three take patience and caring. And if you don't think those are important when it comes to sexiness, I know some Neanderthals who are just dying to meet you.

—And, huggable. Next to cuddle-able and snuggle-able, a sexy woman is completely huggable.

Talking about huggable, isn't it amazing how so many women are named "Mommy"? Doesn't it get confusing? "Romantic Mommy" probably thought so when she asked . . .

Q. How can a parent, without spending zillions on a babysitter, enjoy romance without an audience? My husband and I like intimate candlelight dinners and breakfast in bed, but so do our eight-year-old girl and five-year-old boy. What can we do?

A. To answer this question I went straight to the experts—other mommies. This is what they suggested:

—Dinner for Two—in Miniature. In order to set up an intimate dinner for two in a hungry family of five, one wife told me how she would prepare a miniature romantic dinner for her children and then let them eat in the back of the house while she and her husband nibbled by candlelight in the dining room. The miniature dinner, a massive dessert, and stern instructions to leave Mommy and Daddy alone guaranteed the couple a few hours of uninterrupted intimacy.

—Munchkin Waiters. In what could be the nearly perfect solution to this problem, one couple engaged the services of their early teen-aged daughter as a waitress for their evening repast. After this success, their eight-year-old son asked for a chance to serve and, according to his mother, he did an exceptional job—except for "one small incident with the tomato catsup."

—Itsy-Bitsy DJ. Looking for some way to sit back and

18

enjoy a quiet evening for two, a mommy revealed that she and her husband would select several hours of their favorite tunes from their record collection and then would let their young son act as DJ and play them while they cuddled and listened (away from little eyes) on the back porch.

—Videotape Victory. In a thoroughly modern approach, one parent told me that she guarantees an evening of uninterrupted romance by buying an "eight-pound bag" of popcorn and renting a videotape player and a half-dozen feature-length movies—for her sons. Then, while the boys are having a film festival, she and her hubby can privately enjoy the coming attractions.

—Pac Man Mania. One cunning mommy suggested that, if your child is a video game nut, you should try this: One weekend night when he or she is playing Pac Man on your home set, just mention in passing, "Did you hear that Johnny (or whoever) up the street's highest score is 1,322,417?" Then, just smile and walk away. As long as the electricity holds up, you should be guaranteed a complete evening of privacy. (Muncha, muncha, muncha.)

—Playground Picnic. After taking their two children to elementary school, one couple I know will regularly play hookey from work and enjoy a picnic breakfast in the far corner of the playground. "There are almost no children out at that time of the morning so it's very nice," revealed the mother. But she goes on to warn, "If you have to use the facilities, I suggest you stay away from the children's restrooms. Those midget toilets are murder."

Once the children are asleep (or you just think they are), the romantic possibilities are almost limitless. Instead of just participating in the number one contact sport—you guessed it—here are a few suggestions for adding a little playful romance to your bedroom:

—The Romantic Tuck-in. Taking a clue from your childhood, try tucking-in your partner for a pleasant change of pace. (Don't forget to include a teddy bear, or a bare teddy.) Then, cuddle closely and read your loved one a favorite bedtime story. This is a sure-fire warm-fuzzy romantic event.

—Bedroom Tycoon. Would you like to be fabulously rich and entertained beyond your wildest dreams? You might come close by playing a late-night game of Monopoly in bed. All the rules are the same except for a few special changes which allow for "creative" trading.

—Shark Island. I remember as a child being scared to the point of embarrassment by a game called "Shark Island." It's played by huddling together in the middle of the bed—in absolute darkness—and yabbering until you convince youself that exactly four zillion and three sharks are surrounding you. Only recently have I discovered that, with minor modifications, this is an exceptional game for adults. I'm sure, once you think about it, you can learn to enjoy this game, too.

—And the Family Camp-in. If you would like to involve your whole family in your playful pursuits, try holding a camp-out for the whole gang in your bedroom. Pup tents can be fashioned out of sheets and chairs and moonlight can be provided by a well-placed flashlight. Songs around the camp-stereo, marshmallows semiroasted over an open light bulb, and a midnight bear attack (with Mommy in the starring role) are definitely recommended.

Enough wholesomeness. It's time to ask . . .

Q. What does a man *really* like? I've been looking for a romantic gift for my husband and I haven't a clue. Before I cop-out and buy him another gallon of after-shave (Eau de

20

Sweatsocks) or a pair of edible underwear, *help!*—"Not-So-Gifted Wife"

A. If you can't afford to have your husband served breakfast in bed by the Dallas Cowboy Cheerleaders—his coronary care bill alone would be murder—you might want to try a few of these incredibly romantic, but cheap, ideas.

1) The Love Jar. No, this has nothing to do with Vaseline. It's a touching, creative, and mess-free gift, as Sharon explained: "Last year I wanted to make my husband something really special, as our finances had been cut drastically by cutbacks at his job. I considered all sorts of crafts and decided instead on a 'Love Jar.' I sat down and thought up one hundred different reasons why I loved my husband, wrote each one on a little slip of paper, folded it up, and put them all into a decorative glass jar. Now, once a day, my husband pulls one out at random and is instantly reminded just how truly special he is to me."

2) Designer Romance. One romantic woman used a little needling to show her husband she cares. Here's his letter: When I met my wife I was a very button-down, conservative dresser, so it was a big moment when I got jeans for the first time. It was important to her, but what made it special to me was that after I got them, she stitched the words, 'Love Ya!' on the INSIDE where I could be reminded of her feelings every time I put them on." (And took them off, no doubt.)

3) No Buttons, but Bows. Gloria also found that clothes (or lack of them) make the romantic. "For thirty-three years on his birthday and other special occasions my husband got *me* as a present—naked except for two big bows tied for him," she wrote. Lucky thing they didn't live in Alaska.

4) Romantic Gift Certificates. What do you give your hubby when you have absolutely zilch free time for shopping

and even less money? (Hint: The answer is not "an all-expense-paid trip to the garbage.") You give him a dozen or so romantic gift certificates.

Just swipe a few sheets of your kid's construction paper and write "Darling, I.O.U. _____." Here are a few suggestions for filling in that blank:

1) A handful of his favorite massage oil—expertly applied.

2) A scoop of his favorite ice cream—apply it any way you want to.

3) A game of bubble-bath volleyball.

4) A midnight swim—formal wear is not required. (If you don't have a pool, ask to use your neighbor's . . . afterwards.)

5) An afternoon of horseback riding. If you don't have horses nearby, grab a roll of quarters and kick the kids off the one at the supermarket.

6) A luxurious shampoo. Attack him with a tube of Prell.

7) A not-so-luxurious water fight. What else do you think that high-pressure nozzle on your hose is for?

8) A shopping spree. But, make sure you write, "You take me."

9) One afternoon of yard work. (Like "heavy-duty" tanning.)

10) A post-adolescent pajama party.

11) An evening of dancing. He pays, you lead.

12) A mystery getaway to a romantic rendezvous.

(Translation: "We check in as Mr. and Mrs. Smith for an evening at the No-Tell Motel.")

13) A gift copy of a steamy book like, "The Joy of Pennzoil."

14) An hour (or more) totally alone. Remind him that

this might be accomplished more easily if he were to treat you (and the children) to a movie.

15) An hour totally alone—together. One mother suggested, jokingly I'm sure, that this could only be accomplished by putting the children in Hefty bags. This is not recommended.

16) Your choice of television programs. This is especially handy (for him) when your cultural event ("Robert Redford Plays Kazoo in the Nude at Carnegie Hall") conflicts with his "Battle of the Network Bikinis."

17) A fabulous foot massage. "This little piggy went to market, this little piggy stayed home, and this little piggy went through the ceiling . . ."

18) A romantic business lunch. Make sure you clear all of your afternoon appointments.

19) A car wash. See number seven above.

20) A complimentary back scrub.

21) A strawberries-and-champagne festival. (If you think this a little much, bag the strawberries.)

22) A chocolate-chip-cookie festival. Make enough for a dozen friends, and then don't invite them.

23) An evening at the video arcade. Grab that joystick.

24) A shoulder to cry on, and

25) A shoulder to sigh on.

And last, but certainly not least, what do you do when your husband appears to be suffering from wanderlust? "Puzzled in Plantation, Florida," wanted to know when she wrote . . .

Q. Recently I went to a bar with my husband and one of his friends. Whenever they saw a nice-looking girl walk by, they would turn and smile *big* smiles at each other. It really made me mad. Should I ignore it or should I tell my husband that I don't like him to do that around me?

A. Some spouses have a not-so-subtle way of telling their partners that they're upset: They divorce them.

Instead of this drastic approach, try the following five-point romance repair plan.

1) Decide exactly why your husband's roving eye makes you angry. You might feel that his actions are saying, "I'm tired of you and I'm looking for a little extramarital adventure." Or it might just be that you'd like him, and rightfully so, to pay a little more attention to *you*. Whatever the situation, you first need to know exactly what's bugging you.

2) Whatever you're feeling, tell your husband. Ignoring a problem, no matter how little, is a lot like chug-a-lugging a pitcher of beer—even if you can do it, keeping it bottled up inside you quickly becomes very painful.

If you don't believe me, listen to Evelyn: "My husband recently retired and for a while he would 'help' me at home by recleaning what I had already cleaned. Though he truly did it as a favor, it drove me crazy. Finally, I asked him to stop, and he did. It may sound silly, but his stopping probably saved our marriage." And probably saved Evelyn from being convicted of vacuum-icide.

3) Don't forget romance. It can work wonders, as Leslie discovered. "Every growing relationship has serious moments when subjects that aren't always pleasant need to be discussed. When my man and I have times like these, he holds my hand, no matter how upset we might be. This shows he loves and cares for me and tells me he isn't going to let me go easily. That is Romance!"

4) And don't forget positive reinforcement. If your husband changes his behavior for you, show him that you appreciate it. It works.

Here's one husband's story: "My wife told me that she wanted me to spend more time at home with her and the kids. Reluctantly, I canceled some scheduled overtime and arranged to spend the entire three-day weekend with my family. When I went back to work on Monday, I found in my briefcase a thank-you note from my wife and one from each of my children. They were thanking me for the fun we had together. More than anything else, those notes showed me that a loving family is more important than any job."

5) Be prepared to listen, too. As ranchers say, when the cow beefs, you can bet on what's going to come out of the bull. Expect this—and *listen*. A sincere discussion is a vital part of a healthy and romantic relationship.

Now that you've jump-started your husband, let's see what he can do for you in Chapter 2.

2

"After Seven Years of Marriage, My Wife Just Told Me That I'm B-O-R-I-N-G. What Can I Do?"

Boring husbands (and wives) are yawning across the country in epidemic numbers. To find out if you're a romantic snooze-junky, take the following diagnostic test.

Question One: My idea of a "hot" evening is:

a) Flying to Paris with my spouse for dinner and dancing at Maxim's.

b) Spending a weekend with my partner doing field research for the latest edition of *The Joy of Sex*.

c) Sending out for pizza and watching videotapes of the last eleven Superbowls.

Question Two: When my spouse says, "Darling, come here and give me a hug," I respond by:

a) Enveloping her in a tender embrace.

b) Holding her close to me and whispering, "I love you."

c) Giggling until Moosehead beer comes out my nose.

Question Three: After making love to my partner, I:

a) Caress her gently.

b) Hold her softly for hours.

c) Turn the game back on to see what I've missed in the last thirty-seven seconds.

If you answer *a* or *b* to each of these questions, you're well on your way to being one of the World's Greatest Romantics. If you answered *c* to any, or all, of these questions, you're lucky to be alive.

No matter what you answered, here's a list of ten romantic resolutions to help you become the electrifying jump-starter you were meant to be:

1) Resolve to tell your loved one, "I love you," frequently and openly. When you love someone, it's no time to hide your emotions. Let your loved one know how you feel. At the very least, she will realize that you have great taste in people.

2) Resolve to lose an argument (or two). Arguments can be good for a relationship. Losing one can be great. When you're stuck fighting over some unimportant—but energetic—point, go ahead and give in. You'll both come out winners.

3) Resolve to hold your loved one just for the romance of it. My votes for the best verbs in the English language go to "hold, hug, snuggle, and cuddle." And these verbs are apt to lead to an even more exciting activity—love.

4) Resolve to "feel," and I don't mean groping with your loved one (although that might not be a bad idea). I mean feel free to be emotional. Real men might not eat quiche, but they certainly are not afraid to laugh, love, or cry.

5) Resolve to take chances. Would your loved one like to be kidnaped and spirited away for a night of passion? Would she like to receive flowers just for the heck of it? Would your spouse like to try something intimate and daring? You'll never know unless you try.

6) Resolve to do something *just* for your loved one. One of the best ways to show you care is to make her a promise and keep it. Promise to stop smoking. Promise to share the housework. Promise not to call your mother-in-law "that old Buick." Whatever you promise, *do it*. Why? Just because you love her.

7) Resolve to remember the "little things." Little things like a hug before work or a secret smile during dinner say more than a store-bought gift ever will. Expensive diamonds are for jewelers. Little things are for lovers.

8) Resolve to make a "private and personal" romantic resolution. Every couple knows some secret area in which their relationship can use a little help. Decide what that area is and then resolve to improve it.

9) Resolve to dream. There is a very fine line between reality and fantasy. Take your lover's hand and cross it.

10) And resolve to ask yourself, "How can I be romantic today?" If there is one suggestion that is guaranteed to improve your love life, this is it. Take a moment each day to add the romance your relationship deserves and banish the "B-O-R-I-N-G's" forever.

Now that you've resolved to be trustworthy, loyal, helpful, friendly, courteous, kind, obedient (given a little creative persuasion), cheerful, thrifty, brave, clean, and a whole lot more fun in general, it's time to answer a few of the specific questions you may have. Like this one . . .

Q. What makes a man sexy? Hugh Hefner says it's smoking a pipe and dressing in a mauve silk bathrobe all day. (I could just see wearing that to the plant.) What do you think?—"Not a Playboy, Just a Good Husband"

A. Outside of assorted bunnies, the only people who think Hef is sexy are other men. Hugh, I'd be worried if I were you.

What really makes a man sexy? Here's a view from the other side by Frances, a self-described "mature woman." The characteristics she finds sexy in a man are:

"*Warmth.* The gleam in his eye when he *really* looks at you; the way he lightly touches your arm when he talks to you.

"*Sense of Humor.* He laughs from the belly with his head thrown back; he laughs at himself and *with* you.

"*Openness and Honesty.* He says what he thinks and he means what he says. He shares how he feels.

"*Sensitivity.* Not just for himself, but for others, and he's not afraid that if his sensitivity shows it will label him effeminate.

"*Nurturing.* He knows how and when to care for others; he judiciously offers care only when needed; he is not overprotective.

"*Self-Care.* A sexy man takes care of himself: physically, emotionally, and economically.

"*Faith.* And a sexy man believes that romantic love can last a lifetime and he won't be satisfied with anything less."

Experts agree that to improve the sexual aspects of your relationship (and most other areas as well), you also have to improve communication. You probably already know this and may be wondering . . .

Q. How do I let my partner know what I want in our relationship? How can I improve our communication?—"Tight-Lipped Romantic"

A. The best place to go for improving communication skills is to the experts—qualified, professional counselors who deal with marital relationships.

Just for the fun of it, you might also want to try the

following romance communication game, "Gee, I Didn't Know You Liked Bubble Baths, Too."

Here's how it works. First, you take a piece of paper and make two sets of five flash cards. Next, you number each set of cards from 1 to 5. Then you sit across from each other and, using the flash cards (like at a gymnastics meet), you rate the following fifty romantic activities according to this scale:

1) Need about as much as a case of frostbite.

2) Better than watching "Love Boat" reruns.

3) Important, but the earth doesn't move.

4) Like it even better than my favorite gourmet ice cream.

5) Earthquake city. So much fun it should be illegal.

Pay particular attention to what your partner rates a "5." Then try to see if, together, you can experience the upper limits of the romantic Richter scale.

Here are the activities:

PHYSICAL ROMANCE

1) Cuddling
2) Hugging (even in public)
3) Kissing—especially tenderly
4) Being pampered
5) Nibbling—on the neck
6) Nibbling—behind the ears
7) Nibbling—behind the knees
8) Nibbling—go ahead and surprise me
9) Gentle caressing
10) Back massage
11) Head and neck massage
12) Foot massage
13) Holding hands
14) Exploring fantasies

15) Pillow fights
16) Tickle fights
17) Pillow and tickle fights
18) Trying something *different*
19) Going for a walk
20) Going for broke

EMOTIONAL ROMANCE

21) Time alone
22) Time together
23) Hearing "I love you"
24) Hearing "I need you"
25) Having someone who'll listen
26) Feeling sexy and wanted
27) Feeling independent
28) Feeling intelligent
29) Being best friends, too
30) Being faithful

TRADITIONAL ROMANCE

31) Flowers
32) Candy
33) Cold cash
34) Hot bubble baths
35) Breakfast in bed
36) Picnics
37) Talks together
38) Dreaming together
39) Dinners by candlelight
40) Dessert by no light

ACTIVE ROMANCE

41) Being wild and crazy

42) Being dull and boring
43) Romance-ercise—hug, one, two, three . . .
44) Slow dancing
45) Fast dancing
46) Holding each other and pretending we're dancing
47) Sports (be creative)
48) Catching a concert
49) Going to the movies
50) Going to the supermarket

Now that you have all this nifty information, it's time to put it to work. Here's a weekly schedule for romantics, like "Aerobics Lover," who wonders . . .

Q. Do you have any suggestions for being romantic and losing a little weight at the same time? I know you're not the Richard Simmons of Romance, but any help would be appreciated. P.S. I hate to sweat.

A. Why do I have the sneaking suspicion that people who *love* to sweat also love to eat Volkswagens for lunch? For us non-car-nivores, here's a nearly sweat-free Romance-ercise plan to get you both jump-starting:

Monday. The exercise for today is sit-ups. Lie on your back, bend your knees, have your partner hold your feet, and begin. Try to do two. (You don't want to be overly amazing so early in the week.) Once you've both finished your sit-ups, your Romance-ercise is to bundle up and take a leisurely walk. As Mimi pointed out, walks are a great way to keep you and your relationship healthy. "My husband and I have been taking walks together for nearly forty years. Nothing stops us. If it gets too cold or too hot, we just go to the big shopping malls and walk there. Lots of couples used to take walks. Smart ones still do."

Tuesday. Jogging is the exercise for today. Suit up in your

33

best running togs and take a few laps around your living room. After this strenuous exercise, it's time to Romance-ercise with a relaxing massage. Dorothy tells how: "Take a little baby oil and about an hour and forty-five minutes of your time and give each other a good rub. It is good for your hands and your loved one, and, best of all, it's practically free. Talk to each other the whole time, but *don't* discuss problems."

Wednesday. You're going to love doing push-ups today. Lie on your stomach on the floor next to your partner and go for it. Count to *one*. Then get up, take a shower, get dressed, and go dancing. If you can't find that perfect night spot, do what Nick does. "I love to dance, but I hate bars," he wrote. "So several times a month I'll put some nice music on the stereo and dance at home with my wife. I'm not a great dancer, but whatever we do is just between her, me, and the stereo—if you know what I mean."

Thursday. How long has it been since you've ridden a bicycle? That's what I thought. So, instead of taking a spin on the real thing, today's exercise involves lying on your back on your bed and pedaling your legs in the air. After about thirteen seconds of pumping, it's time to Romance-ercise by cuddling with your partner. I'll leave the rest of today's exercise up to you.

Friday. Get ready, because today's the day you pump iron. Grab a massive hunk of metal, like a pocket stapler, and lift it over your head ten times. After catching your breath, it's time to exercise your appetite. This dinner plan was suggested by Mary: "Our favorite romantic evening is putting our two sons to bed a little early and having a nice, peaceful dinner. We never have anything too fancy since our budget is tight, but we enjoy a warm loaf of bread, some cheese, fresh vegetables, and a bottle of wine. I never do the

34

dishes—we just carry our wine glasses into the living room, light a few candles, and talk. This has become a beautiful and important part of our lives."

Saturday. Some people hold marathons on Saturdays. Others hold tennis matches. Romance-ercise fans hold hands, as Edna revealed: "I married a man of few words, but full of kindness and gentleness. Just once before we were married he told me he loved me and he could look at me forever. That was fifty-five years ago. The words he doesn't say are expressed when we sit at night together on the davenport and he holds and squeezes my hand, and at night when we go to sleep holding hands. To me this is the greatest of love."

And *Sunday.* Today is the day you do as little, or as much, as you want—*together.*

Do romance and sports mix? We've already seen that romantic exercise is no sweat, but what if you're wondering . . .

Q. What can I do? My wife says that she's a sports widow. Sure, I like golf, but she doesn't play. What do you suggest? Hurry—she's threatened to do strange things to my putter.—"Husband of Teed-Off in Tucson"

A. Golf has been called a great way to ruin an otherwise pleasant walk. And an obsession with this sport, or any other, is a great way to ruin an otherwise pleasant relationship.

Before she gets weird with your clubs, try this: Invite her out to the course—even if she doesn't play—for a leisurely nine holes. Make sure that she fully understands the meaning of the word "Fore!" and that losing thirty or more balls on the first few holes is to be expected.

Once you've completed your round, go to the clubhouse,

buy a couple of cold beers and some sandwiches, and head out to the area by the tenth tee for a quickie picnic. She, you, and your putter should be very happy.

Of course, you could also try a few sports that you could really play *together.* Here are several that are guaranteed to get your romantic blood pumping.

Swimming. Stroke, stroke, stroke. Johnny Weismuller and Esther Williams knew a good thing when they saw it.

Kite Flying. All right, so it's not in the Olympics . . . yet.

Touch Football. I think the name pretty well sums it up.

Scuba or *Skin Diving.* Think of the possibilities.

Snow Skiing. I'm heartily in favor of any sport whose major attraction is warming up afterwards.

Backgammon. You know what they say, pain is gain.

Bicycle-Built-for-Two-ing. You can actually rent these things in most cities. Check your Yellow Pages.

Bowling. Bowling has had a bad romantic reputation ever since Ralph Cramden used to do it on "The Honeymooners." Try it. I think you'll like it.

And *Sailing.* Nothing, and I mean nothing, beats sailing for pure romantic fun. If you don't have a lake or ocean nearby—build one.

(NOTE TO JUMP-STARTERS: The following sports are definitely *not* recommended if your relationship is less-than-perfect: Fencing, javelin throwing, karate, judo, sky diving, mountain climbing, lacrosse, and darts.)

Now that you've engaged in a number of romantic activities and sports, it's time to come clean. Bubble baths are a perfect way to do this, but, as "In Hot Water" wrote, you might not know how.

Q. I've read a number of times about "elegant" bubble

baths (which I'm sure I'd enjoy), but my bathroom is the pits. I can't afford to replace everything, and I was wondering if you had any suggestions to help me out.

A. Even the pitsiest of bathrooms—yours included—can, with a little creative preparation, host the most romantic and elegant of bubble baths. Here's a seven-point plan designed to get the most out of your B-U-B-B-L-E-S.

B—*Be* daring. There are few relationships that cannot be jump-started by a bubble bath picnic, a bubble bath ice cream festival, a bubble bath and champagne party, an evening of bubble bath caressing, or my favorite, an hour of bubble bath snuggling. Believe me, there is more to a simple bubble bath than meets the eye.

U—*Use* plenty of elbow grease. Ring around your romance is not recommended. If you haven't cleaned your tub since last Arbor Day (men, pay attention to this), *clean it now.* As far as the rest of the bathroom goes, do your best and remember that dim candlelight can hide a multitude of sins.

B—*Bubbles,* bubbles, and more bubbles. The elegance of a bubble bath is directly proportional to the amount of bubbles. Don't assume that the little packet of bubble bath given to your family six Christmases ago by Aunt Mathilda is going to fill your bathroom with foam—it won't.

Instead, try to find a bottle of liquid bubble bath with a scent you find appealing (avoid anything marked "Industrial Strength"). Some stores even sell long-lasting unscented bubble bath—you provide that extra touch by adding a few drops of your favorite perfume or cologne.

B—*Be* creative. Bring in your stereo (or just the speakers) and surround yourselves with romantic music. Remember to position these, or anything electrical, as far from the water as possible. A 110-volt shock is probably not the kind of stimulation you had in mind.

Also you may want to separate your bubble bath from the rest of the bathroom with a screen divider. Shower curtains are fine, but screens add a touch of romance (and help prevent onslaughts of curtain claustrophobia).

L—*Lights* are out. Candlelight is in. If there is room, place one sturdily supported candle on a corner of your tub. This provides just the right amount of softly diffused light for any bubble bath activity, except for heavy reading.

If the candle won't fit there, place one or two candles in secure holders elsewhere in your bathroom. Make sure you keep them away from flammables like curtains.

E—*Enjoy* a little liquid refreshment—champagne, chilled white wine, sparkling soda on ice—while you bubble. In addition, why not nibble on fresh strawberries, seedless grapes, or earlobes for that added romantic touch?

S—*Sit* back and enjoy. Once you've finished all the preparations, it's time to let romance do the work.

And speaking about bathrooms, did you know that this smallest room in your house can be the cause of some of the biggest jump-starting difficulties? Believe it. Here's a question I received from "A Furious Wife" . . .

Q. I need you to settle a controversy for me. Last night I groggily got up and headed for the bathroom where I nearly killed myself when I fell *into* the john—my husband had left the seat up again. Now, a soggy seat is bad enough, but this was the last straw. Where do you stand on this issue: up or down?

A. Your husband should sit corrected. Without a doubt, it is the duty of *both* parties—husbands, this means you—to leave the bathroom seat down after use. Dry would be nice, too.

This is but one of the many pressing issues facing couples

38

today. Here are a few more.

—The Toothpaste Tube. Rolled or flattened? While I'm sure Congress is looking into this one, the romantics I surveyed picked "flattened." Even when you succeed in rolling a tube of toothpaste, your only reward is a handful of the stuff through a crack. Flattening may be "declassé," but it works.

—Playing Post Office. Should you open your partner's mail or not? Have you ever wondered why a letter opener is considered a deadly weapon? Everyone agreed that you should never, and that's *never,* open your partner's mail unless specifically requested. A handful of paper cuts to the person who does.

—The Battle of the Bedroom. Who makes the bed? One couple suggested that the husband makes the bed Monday, Wednesday, and Friday, while the wife makes the bed Tuesday, Thursday, and Saturday. On Sunday, this couple said they make something else.

—Garbage Wars. Who takes out the trash? Most women believed that men should consider this an exciting form of body building. Most men believed that women should welcome this "return to nature." I believe that these couples should trash their differences and get a compacter.

—And That Sinking Feeling. Who should do the dishes? Everybody threw in the towel on this one, except one wise woman who suggested romantics should make something less messy for dinner—reservations.

Of course, not all arguments can be settled this easily. Some arguments can only be settled after much time, patient effort, and emergency medical treatment. The question is . . .

Q. How do we get over the argument so that we can get

39

to the good stuff—like making up afterwards?

A. Experts and successful couples agree that arguments (except fatal ones) can play a healthy role in a relationship. How do you get over one? Simple. You *concede.*

Here are a few ideas for losing in style.

1) *Before* the big event, take the time to write an "Open in Case of Argument" letter to your spouse. In it you should write of your love and affection and of the many things you cherish about your life-long companion. (Avoid any reference to "Your money.")

This valuable letter should be written on heavy-duty paper—to withstand repeated use—and should be placed where you can get to it *quickly.*

2) Some arguments take more than just an apology. They take bribery. Instead of laying out cold cash, prepare a special "I Care" package for your wife.

In it you can place a few special pictures from your courtship (like a photo of your spouse getting sick on your honeymoon cruise), an old love letter (preferably not from someone else), a selection of candy and chocolate, a romantic book (B. Kliban's *Never Eat Anything Bigger Than Your Head* comes to mind), or a not-yet-cancelled credit card.

3) In the heat of an argument it is amazingly easy to forget some very important things—like why you got married in the first place. To improve your memory (and to make it easier to apologize) make a list—during a happy moment—of all the reasons why you got married. (Come on, now. You can think of more than two.)

Then, in the midst of fury, lock yourself in the bathroom and read it. If nothing else, it might give you a good laugh.

4) And if you can't face apologizing in person, you can always:

—Send a mailgram. Just call Western Union and charge

it to your telephone. Your note will arrive the nex
bill will arrive in about a month.

—Record your message on a cassette and lea
loved one. You might also want to add some appr....
music, like that country and western classic, "You've Been
Flushed from the Bathroom of My Heart." Sound effects
might be nice, too.

—Or, write your apology on the bathroom mirror with
soap. Nothing beats a little good, clean fun.

So, when the time for your next argument arrives as
scheduled, don't worry. Just remember the words of the wise
woman talking about her husband, "Believe me, when we
argue it doesn't mean I don't love him. It just means that I
love him loudly."

Now that these vital issues have been resolved and you
and your wife are back on speaking terms, it's time to be
suave, debonair, and glib. (Well, you can try, can't you?)
"Married to a Southern Mush-Mouth" tried to be when he
asked . . .

Q. My wife told me that I don't pay enough "mushy"
attention to her. Hell, we've got six kids—isn't that enough?
Do you have any suggestions? I'm not very good at kissy-
face.

A. Every relationship must have a good dose of mush
now and then. In fact, you're lucky that your mushless wife
has not yet told you to play "kissy" with her grits.

How do you make mush? One of the best ways is to give
your wife honest and sincere compliments when appropriate.
Before you think that all compliments are just fake flattery,
consider this: What do you think when someone compliments you on your appearance or on a job well done?

No, you don't think, "This person probably sells real

41

estate.'' You think, "Obviously, this person is a highly intelligent and perceptive human being."

We need sincere flattery. It's nice to know when someone else thinks you're wonderful. And it's wonderful to let someone else know they're nice, too. Here are a few hints.

Physical Compliments. I don't know anyone who gets tired of hearing, "You have beautiful eyes," or "Your hair is gorgeous." The trick in making a compliment really special is to be as specific as romantically possible. If you like her eyes, mention the color (and no, not "red"). If you love her hair, tell her why. Is it incredibly soft? Does it smell like lilacs? Do you like the way it fits into a box at night?

And, don't be afraid to be a little out-of-the-ordinary. Tell your wife her earlobes drive you wild or let her know how tasty the backs of her knees are.

Warm-Fuzzy Compliments. Everybody also likes to hear how outstandingly intelligent and talented he or she is. The problem, according to many people, is that few others are intelligent enough to notice.

Well, you don't have to be a genius to tell your wife that you like how organized she is, how smart she is, or how wonderful she makes you feel.

I Love You Compliments. There is only one phrase that beats, "I love you." It's "I love you because _____." Because you are so tender. Because you understand. Because you're everything I've always hoped for.

"Is This a Compliment?" Compliment. Then again, there are some compliments better left unsaid. Some of these are:

—"All this fat makes you so-o-o cuddly."

—"You remind me of a dog I used to have."

—"Did you know you look just like 'Tootsie' in the movies?"

—"My wife. I think I'll keep you."

—"I like you even better than broccoli."

—"I don't think your chin looks like a venetian blind."

—"You know, all those wrinkles give you character."

—"Nice blouse. Wasn't that in style last year?"

—"Wow. You haven't been real bitchy in at least a week."

—And, "Your diet may have failed miserably, but I still think you're swell."

Honestly, the best compliment you can give to someone is to share your life with them. This brings up the age-old question . . .

Q. Does romance have to die when you get older? I'm still ready, but my spouse pooped out when our Packard did. Is this the way it has to be?

A. No, a hundred years, no. Romance is not just for the young, it's for the young at heart. Here are just a few letters from lovers who have no intention of retiring:

—"What's wrong with romance and older people?" asked Doris. "Nothing, as far as I can see. I've found myself a gentleman and he is a *gentle* man. He is sixty-eight years young and I'm fifty-six. Petting is not just for kids. Think about it."

—Joan agreed and wrote, "Romantic things are not just for the young. We middle-agers are in it also. After many years of wedded bliss, I still write a small love note and put it in his lunch bag every day. On Fridays I always write something extra, hints on what to expect over the weekend. He loves it! Our love life is never dull."

—"Let nobody tell you love and romance can't happen to us 'older' people," warned "Very Happy in Utah." "I recently married and I'm sixty-five—my spouse is sixty-eight. The love, excitement, and, yes, sex is as wonderful as it was at age eighteen. Every day holds something very special. We marvel that it could happen to us. Young people may wonder that older people can fall in love and they may not really believe it. But, believe me, it's true.''

—And even when it comes to dealing with death (and it's tough to get older than that), romance lives on, as Judy explained: ''My parents are crazy—crazy in love. When they wrote their teen-age love notes to each other, they always included a little hand-drawn heart with their initials 'M and M' (Minnie and Melvin). Now they have done the most crazy, romantic thing I can think of. This year they purchased a tombstone for their long-owned cemetery lot. Yes, you guessed it—it covers both graves and is beautifully engraved with a big heart and two big *M*'s cuddled close inside. They have been married over forty years and still think 'Romance lasts forever.'''

While Minnie and Melvin are getting ready to go to a better place, some couples are just trying to get out of town. ''Better Late than Never,'' for example . . .

Q. My wife and I were married just over two years ago, but we've never had a chance to go on a honeymoon. Now, we're finally going to do it. I think I already have a good idea what to do when we get to our hotel (I've got the champagne and bubble bath ready), but I'm wondering if you have any romantic suggestions for the flight there?

A. In-flight romance can be pretty exciting. (Calm down—that's not what I meant—and besides, have you ever tried getting two people into one of those tiny restrooms? It's almost impossible.)

Here are a few stimulating *and* wholesome ideas:

—Bring on board a small gift-wrapped present (hidden

from your spouse, not the security guards) in a coat pocket or bag. It could be a box of candy, an intimate airmail love letter, a bottle of perfume, a piece of jewelry, a pair of car keys (not the car, just the keys), or a cute stuffed animal. Then, excuse yourself for a moment, track down a flight attendant, and *ask* him or her to deliver your gift. (Remember flight attendants are *very* busy people. They'll do their best to help you, but if they can't, don't get upset—just smile and deliver the gift yourself.)

—You can use the same approach to deliver flowers while in flight. A small bouquet of trimmed sweetheart roses fits nicely into a gift-wrapped shoe box.

—Romantic music is a vital part of any romantic event (and a great way to calm the worries of white-knuckle flyers). Since your normal symphony orchestra is pretty tough to cram into a carry-on bag, you might want to bring along a portable cassette player with dual headphones. Any favorite music is great, but classical tapes add just the right amount of, well, class.

—And clever romantics can bring along their own bottle of bubbly for a high-flying romantic treat—but be prepared for the results. I understand giggling is greatly intensified at ten thousand feet.

Even after you've touched down, your romance can still soar. Try these hints for excitement in the airport:

—Break away from your loved one in the terminal for a moment, find a telephone, and then have her paged. She'll have fun wondering, "Gosh. Who knows me in Lubbock?"

—For a reasonable, but not inexpensive sum, you can have a telegram sent to the airport ticket counter before you arrive at your destination. Address it to your spouse. A simple, "DEAREST DARLING. STOP. I LOVE YOU. DON'T STOP," might be fun.

—Flowers can also be sent to a far-flung ticket counter for later pick-up. Just call a florist ahead of time and bill it to your credit card. Make sure you get your travel details right or your partner could end up with a handful of compost.

—And daring husbands can surprise their wives by calling ahead to the airport restaurant, making reservations, and ordering an intimate dinner for two over the phone. (Payment, again, can be handled with plastic.)

Your wife may call you many things after this, but I'll bet "boring" won't be one of them.

3

"I Really Like My Boyfriend, but If We Go Out to Jack-in-the-Box and a Movie One More Time, I Think I'll Puke. What Else Can We Do?"

One sure way to induce romantic nausea is to bang around in a nonromantic rut. Fortunately for queasy rut-runners, jump-starting works even better than Pepto-Bismol and soda crackers combined.

Here's an entire year of fun, exciting, and easily digestible jump-starting suggestions guaranteed to get you out of Jack's bathroom and into your romance.

THE OFFICIAL JUMP-STARTERS' CALENDAR

JANUARY

Week 1 National "Jump-Start Me" Week
—Pin this slogan on your blouse and go see your boyfriend.
Week 2 This Week Kicks Off the International Bad Ice Skating Season
—At the very least, this will make your loved one fall for you.
Week 3 Do Something Classy on Sunday

—Rent two tuxedos and go bowling.

Week 4 Hold a Polynesian Nibble Festival

    —Samoa? Don't mind if I do.

Week 5 Saturday Is "I'm Dreaming of a Late Christmas" Day

    —Take your partner shopping and see how much money you save when he pays.

FEBRUARY

Week 1 Hold a "97 Days before Our Anniversary" Anniversary

    —So, who's counting?

Week 2 *Valentine's Day*

    —Don't just send a card, send Romance. Mail your partner a picnic.

Week 3 Surprise Your Loved One with a "Hot-Buttered Whatever" Weekend

    —Hot-buttered rum, hot-buttered popcorn, and hot-buttered whatever else your devilish mind can think of.

Week 4 The 29th Is "Leap on Your Romance Day"

    —Happy landings.

MARCH

Week 1 Return of National Stay in Bed Together Day

    —Totally ignore Monday. It won't mind.

Week 2 "Gee, Is It the New Year Already?" Week

    —Time to finally get to your New Year's resolutions—from *last* year.

Week 3 Enjoy a Drive in the Country This Weekend

    —Explore the native wildlife.

Week 4 Hold a Polar Picnic in the Park

    —Prepare an elegant basket, bundle up, and rub

your romance for warmth.

Week 5 Easter Sunday
—A day for quiet reflection—together.

APRIL

Week 1 Do Something Really Crazy on April Fool's Day
—Hold a pajama party at work.

Week 2 International Dance in the Rain Week
—If it isn't raining, try the shower.

Week 3 Hold a Hibachi Steak Fry
—Bubbly and beef can be a rare experience.

Week 4 Time for a Munchkin Mania Party
—Rent a videotape player and watch *The Wizard of Oz* with a dozen or so of your shortest friends.

Week 5 Get Down with a Country Swing Weekend
—Invite Willie Nelson over (well, almost) and dance until dawn.

MAY

Week 1 National "May I _____ You?" Month
—"May I hug you?" "May I kiss you?" "May I romance you?"

Week 2 Sunday Is Mother's Day
—Flowers, candy, and large unmarked bills are sure to be well-received.

Week 3 National Greek Week
—Take a pound of baklava to a friend.

Week 4 Wednesday Is Global Foot Massage Day
—Be a self-made jump-starter. Start at the bottom and work your way up.

Week 5 Be Kind to Animals Week
—A time to "cherish" beer-drinking boyfriends and hubbies.

JUNE

Week 1 June Is International Picnic Month
—I'll bet you can find 101 fun things to nibble on.

Week 2 Regional Water Sports Week
—Don't forget the Olympic bubble bath volleyball trials.

Week 3 Sunday Is Father's Day
—Time to pamper Daddy (and we're not talking diapers here, either).

Week 4 Get a Designer Tan This Weekend
—Catch some rays in your local shopping mall.

Week 5 This Week Begins the Six Months of Chocolate
—Which immediately follows the Half-Year of Hershey.

JULY

Week 1 Declare Your Romantic Independence on the Fourth
—Sneak off together and set off some private fireworks.

Week 2 Hold a South of the Border Heat Wave Festival
—Fill a wading pool with strawberry margaritas.

Week 3 Thursday Is "Tonight Is Yours" Night
—Enjoy a romantic fantasy.

Week 4 This Is International Cookie Week
—Make enough for a dozen friends—and, again, don't invite them.

Week 5 Friday Is New Year's Eve
—Romantically sponsored by the National Society of Procrastinators.

50

AUGUST

Week 1 August Is Happy Un-Month
—Enjoy a happy un-birthday, a happy un-anniversary, or a happy un-bar-mitzvah.

Week 2 August 14 Is Valentine's Day—The Sequel
—Time to dust off your cupid. Promise you'll be gentle.

Week 3 "Ignore This Week" Week
—Why not cuddle together and sleep through it?

Week 4 National Gone with the Wind Week (All proceeds go to benefit Scarlett Fever.)
—Grab your Rhett and show him where to go and what to do.

Week 5 Friday Is Dieter's Delight Day
—Immediately followed by the annual "Let's Eat Banana Splits until They Come Out of Our Ears" Hour

SEPTEMBER

Week 1 Bring a Friend Dessert Week
—Be sure to make it yourself (wink, wink, nudge, nudge).

Week 2 Hold a Congratulations on Not Winning the Nobel Prize Party
—Invite the president, Chuck and Di, and a few hundred of your closest friends.

Week 3 Test Drive a Schwinn This Weekend
—Watch out for smiling and waving people in Mercedes.

Week 4 Saturday Is Romance and Your Pet Day
—Treat your dog to a bubble bath and massage.

51

Week 5 National Twinkie Week
  —Pack a picnic lunch with these babies.

OCTOBER

Week 1 Hold Your Own Oktoberfest This Month
  —Grab your wienerschnitzel and go for it.
Week 2 Do a Little California Dreaming This Weekend
  —Go surfing in a jacuzzi.
Week 3 Friday Night Catch a Screening of a Classic Motion Picture
  —Like a midnight showing of *The Rocky Horror Picture Show.*
Week 4 Hold a Western Re-Union on Monday
  —Send a creatively cryptic telegram to a friend.
Week 5 The 31st Is Halloween
  —Private costume parties are such fun, it's scary.

NOVEMBER

Week 1 Give Your Loved One a Daisy a Day This Week
  —Try not to reuse the same one.
Week 2 Read Your Partner the Comics This Sunday
  —"Here we see Lucy holding the football for Charlie Brown with Snoopy giggling in the background. . . ."
Week 3 Enjoy Romance and the "Tonight Show" This Friday
  —Turn down the sound and make up your own dialogue.
Week 4 Thanksgiving
  —Be kind to your "turkey" this week.
Week 5 National Aerobics Week
  —Don't forget to do plenty of aerobic cuddling.

DECEMBER

Week 1 Movie Matinee Madness Month
    —Take your sweetheart to the latest Disney flick.
Week 2 Begin the Twelve Days of Christmas
    —Partridges are cute, but messy. Municipal bonds might be nice.
Week 3 Sit on Santa This Week
    —Ho, ho, ho.
Week 4 Christmas
    —Forget a "Mr. Masher-Dasher." It's the little "just for you" things that really count.
Week 5 New Year's Eve
    —Get out your Guy Lombardo records and cuddle until April.

How many of you have been to a *really* fancy restaurant lately? You know, the kind that offers "fine food at reasonable terms." If you're like me and don't enjoy taking your banker with you on an evening out, you're probably wondering . . .

Q. How do you wine and dine someone—and then get change back from your dollar?—"Ronald"

A. You don't—but you can come close. Here are a few suggestions guaranteed to make even fast-food (gag me with a Whopper) a tasty romantic experience.

—Jack-in-the-Box. Instead of just getting a burger (and no, it won't impress your date if you order it "medium-rare") try this: Gift-wrap a small present, like a bottle of perfume or after shave, and drop it off at Jack's *before* your date. Arrange to have the counter attendant secretly place it in your burger bag. (A massive $1.00 tip should do the trick.) Then, give the bag to your partner and watch the excitement

53

when he or she finds a surprise with the fries.

—McDonald's. Using the same general approach, arrange to have a bouquet of flowers presented to your date when you pull up to the drive-thru window. This is one thing that McDonald's has *not* served a billion times.

—Pizza Hut. Did you know that most pizza places, if asked, will arrange the ingredients on your pizza in the shape of a heart? It's true. (In fact, one place told me they've done hearts, initials, and even a "pepperoni Star of David.") Apparently, there's no limit to what some guys can do with a sausage.

In addition, some places will even make pizzas in specialty shapes—initials, flowers, circles, etc.

—Kentucky Fried Chicken. Honest to the Colonel, one romantic told me that he purchased a bucket of chicken and placed a bottle of massage oil in it with a note that said: "Finger lickin' good."

—Dairy Queen. And for dessert, you can give your date a gourmet Dilly Bar with a personal message written on the stick. Something like, "Hurry. I'm melting," might be nice.

If you're absolutely, positively, undeniably against fast-food in any form (10 to 1 you used to work at one of these places) what do you do? You can go out with Betty Crocker or you can ask . . .

Q. How can I have a million-dollar date on a zero-dollar budget? I'm a poor student, but I've got some standards. Can you help?—"Valley Romantic"

A. Have you ever met a "rich" student? I have—both of them—and I'm sure you're a lot more fun. Why? You've got standards, you've got imagination, and you've got this book.

Here's your story: You pick up your date for dinner, dressed in your finest, and whisk her (or him—let's not be

54

sexist here) off to a neighborhood park where, much to your surprise, a chilled bottle of bubbly (7-Up for younger romantics), two glasses, and a linen-covered table await you. From there, you take your date back to your house where a candlelit dinner, complete with tuxedoed waiter, has been prepared. The menu? A crisp tossed salad, baked potato, broccoli in cheese sauce, grilled steak (medium rare), and more bubbly (or 7-Up—vintage: Tuesday).

A fantasy just for the children of J.R. Ewing? Horse-hockey. Here's how you do it.

First, arrange to have one of your school friends place the bottle, glasses, and table in the park on schedule (avoid leaving them for safe-keeping with anyone named "Knuckles").

Next, "convince" another friend to prepare the meal. (Bribery is such a tacky word.) Relax, they don't need a direct line to Julia Child. Baked potatoes and steak are a snap. Broccoli and cheese sauce come in cute little "boilable" pouches these days, and it's pretty tough to seriously maim a salad.

Then, dress up a friend in the closest thing you have to a tuxedo (how about an OP shirt and cords?) and hope he or she isn't a graduate of the Jerry Lewis School for Waiters.

Awesome.

Unlike the days of "Leave It to Beaver," today's "boyfriend-girlfriend" relationships go way beyond what Wally ever dreamed of. Before we get to the details, let's first consider . . .

Q. What do you call a "boy"-friend who's fifty-four years old? I'm a forty-five-year-old single woman. I'm seeing a gentleman friend very regularly and I don't know how to introduce him. Do you have any suggestions?—"Let

Me Introduce Tom, My ?"

A. Romantically speaking, the personal details of your relationship with Tom are really nobody else's business. If you choose to let people know, here are a few suggestions.

—"I'd like you to meet my special friend, Tom."

—"Let me introduce Tom, my friend."

—"Good afternoon, Gladys. This is my Tom."

—Or, better yet, "Mildred, Gladys, this is Tom."

If you're looking for an out-of-the-ordinary *private* name for your partner, you might want to try a few of these gems actually used by readers in their letters to my newspaper column.

—Snookums

—Honeybunch

—Honeypie

—Princess Honeybear

—My Squeeze

—My Huggable, Lovable Man

—Mr. Cuddles

—Mrs. America

—Hubby Hips

—My Little Jacques Cousteau

—My Baby-O-Baby

—Darling Dearest

—My Desire

—Mr. Love

—My Joystick

—My Pet (preferable to My Little Alpo Eater)

—My Little Tax Deduction

—Hunky

—Doc

—Snoozy (this is beginning to sound like the Seven Dwarfs)

—And, Clyde (short for Clydesdale, or so she says)

Now for the thoroughly modern details . . .

Q. My boyfriend and I live in a one-bedroom apartment. While we like romance as much as the next couple, our small space is cramping our style. Short of moving, do you have any suggestions for improving apartment life romance?—"Romance In Apt. 409, Gee"

A. Just because you're short on space doesn't mean you have to be short on romance, too. Here are some ideas to help you "uncramp" your style.

—Apartment laundry rooms are not generally recognized as bastions of romantic excitement, but you can change this. On your next trip to the wash cycle, hide a small picnic lunch at the bottom of the laundry basket (avoid Limburger cheese at all costs). Ask your loved one for assistance with your "heavy" load and then surprise him or her with an intimate meal during the wash cycle. You're sure to turn on more than just the Maytag.

—Apartment mailboxes are perfect places to leave little love notes for your partner. Be sure to address them directly to the intended recipient, however. You wouldn't want to confuse your mailman.

—If you're one of the lucky ones and your apartment has racquetball courts, consider this: Even if you've never swung a racket in your life, you can still score big by surprising your partner with a little candlelight and champagne at center court. You might also want to bring along a piece of paper and some tape to cover that little, but obtrusive, peephole in the door.

—Apartment jacuzzis are perfect for helping your loved one relieve the tensions of the day. There is no better place, almost, for giving and receiving a foot, hand, and shoulder massage. (If the spa is crawling with people, just hop in and loudly ask your partner how his "nasty skin condition" is doing. You should be blissfully alone in seconds.)

—If you feel you lack privacy in your tiny abode, here's a suggestion: Incredibly intimate bed curtains can be made by sewing two king-sized sheets together and attaching them to a two-foot circle of ¼-inch plywood. The circle is then suspended above the head of the bed from a sturdy ceiling plant hanger and the curtains are attached to the bed by just tucking them in or by sewing on dandy little strips of Velcro.

These low-cost curtains are a great way to transform an otherwise blah bedroom into an intimate hideaway. By the way, this is definitely *not* recommended for smokers.

—And, if your roomie arrives home late from work, you can be a pal and save him or her a parking space with strategically placed orange traffic cones. When your apartment manager asks you what you're doing, just smile and mumble something about "national security."

Dreaded "diseases" are great for clearing a jacuzzi, but what do you do when your partner is *really* sick? How do you handle . . .

Q. The flu. My boyfriend has it and it's really interfering with our relationship. What can I do?—"Sick of Sniffle City"

A. Now do you see why your mother always told you to marry a doctor? Nothing, with the possible exception of mothers-in-law, can be more chilling to a relationship than the flu.

To help you get out of Sniffle City, try this seven-point jump-starting prescription:

1) Bring your loved one chicken soup. It may not be original, but it's highly recommended by such career roman-

tics as Liz and Dick, Ozzie and Harriet, and Mr. and Mrs. Campbell. If your boyfriend can't stomach the stuff, try a hot bowl of antihistamines.

2) Avoid mentioning such topics as wills, life insurance policies, and tombstone rentals when talking to your partner. Instead, make sure he has plenty of fluffy pillows and a carton of Kleenex. As one romantic wrote, "My honey was sneezing up a storm and I wanted to make him feel better. After getting him his drugs, I took a roll of toilet paper and wrote little love notes on each square. He thought it was a great idea and didn't even mind that the ink made his nose turn blue."

3) Aches, pains, and sneezing are bad enough, but there is one flu sympton that is even worse—boredom. You can help by bringing your partner plenty of light reading material, like *War and Peace* by Tolstoi or Emile Zola's *L'Assommoir*. If he'd prefer something a little more intellectual, bring him up to date on the latest soaps. ("The guy with the frizzy hair is Luke. He's nice. He used to be Laura's, but she's dead. That other guy is Scorpio. He's *sexy.* And that's Heather. She's a tramp . . .")

4) Little household chores become big household headaches when you're sick. Offer to do the dishes, feed the dogs (before they feed themselves), water the plants, get the mail, and take out the garbage. This is especially recommended for those of you attempting to qualify for sainthood.

5) Those popular portable cassette players are also great for soothing the sickened beast. Just place those little headphones on his head and send him off to slumber land with such tunes as Brahm's "Lullaby," Glenn Miller's "In the Mood," or Ethel Merman's Greatest Hits.

6) Sometimes people can be so sick that even getting to the shower or tub will qualify them for "That's Incredible."

If your partner gets this bad, give him a Florence Nightingale-endorsed sponge bath. Just take a clean sponge (not that moldy one under the bathroom sink), dip it in warm water, squeeze it until it's damp—not dripping—and rub it on your loved one's quivering body. To get full coverage, you'll probably have to repeat this procedure three or four times. For a comforting touch, you might also, as one nurse actually suggested, "Sprinkle baby powder on his back, shoulders, and teenie weenie butt." Honest.

7) And if all of this tender loving care seems to be too much, try this: Make him agree, before you even lift one aspirin, that he'll do the same thing for *you* when you're sick. This isn't un-romantic. It's a tender and touching way for you *both* to show your trust and affection. Just make sure you get it in writing.

And fevers aren't the only way to heat up a relationship. A little mystery can fire things up, too . . .

Q. I'm looking for something exciting to get for my boyfriend (we live together) on his birthday. I've considered singing telegrams and balloon bouquets, but I'd like something a little more special. Besides, he's a pretty private person. Any ideas?—"Romantic Thrill Seeker"

A. When it comes to thrills and chills, no one beats those amazing romantics, Ralph and Thelma. And when it comes to surprising birthdays, nothing beats Ralph's latest as he explains in this mystery novelette:

"I knew I never should've trusted a dame. Those sultry green eyes, those moist puckered lips, those size 14 pumps. Everything about her spelled Trouble.

"It started out as your ordinary 110 degree summer evening. I arrived home late from work—my moped had boiled over. I walked up to the front door and lit a smoke. In the

60

flickering light of the match I saw a sealed envelope taped to the door. 'Open Me, Dummy,' was all it said.

"I opened it. The note it contained was brief and cryptic. 'Put out your cigarette and come inside.' I did.

"Of all the crummy joints in all the crummy neighborhoods, why had she picked mine? I spied another note taped to the coat rack. Her message was subtle: 'Take off your clothes, hang them up, and go to the guest bathroom.' I was on to her little game. I took off my clothes, hung them up, and headed for the guest bathroom.

"Striding naked through the house I was ready for anything. The neighbors waved at me as I passed by the living room window. I wasn't ready for that. I ducked into the bathroom. A note was taped to the shower curtain. 'Take a shower and read the next note,' it said.

"I followed directions, but it was tough to make out the message. The shower was making the ink run. 'Dry off, dab on a little cologne, put on a robe, and meet me in the frrzrp,' it instructed. I couldn't find the frrzrp, so I headed for the bedroom.

"Up until that moment, I thought I'd seen it all. But there, sitting in the middle of the bed was Thelma, dressed in little more than a grin. A platter held cracked crab on ice. A bucket held cold beer. What a dame.

" 'This could be the beginning of a beautiful friendship,' I said. She smiled and pulled my ring tab."

Summer is also a great time to take your partner to a movie. "Big deal," you say. If it isn't, listen to this . . .

Q. I've probably been to the movies a billion times and have done exactly the same things. Do you have any romantic suggestions on how to spice up my life at the theater?— "E.T."

A. Earthlings and extraterrestrials alike can have a great time at the movies, even without phoning home for instructions. Here are three examples of how a simple trip to the theater can become a trip that will make you a star:

—Clark and Lois had been seeing each other for some time, but their relationship had yet to get off the ground. In order to rise above his competition, Clark decided to make the most of their upcoming date.

On the fateful evening he picked up Lois, presented her with a bouquet of flowers, and told her that she looked "keen." During their drive to the theater, he suggested that they go out for ice cream afterwards, "Uh, Lois. Could I ask you what your favorite type of ice cream is—maybe?" probed Clark, both hands firmly on the wheel. "Pralines and cream," she shot back.

At the theater Clark escorted Lois to their seats and then went to buy popcorn. He took a surprising amount of time. "Uh, some guy kicked goobers in my face," Clark explained sheepishly when he returned.

Munching on her popcorn, Lois discovered a surprise. No, it wasn't a goober. It was a gift-wrapped silver necklace with a beautiful rose pendant. "You wonderful sneak, you," Lois squealed. Clark smiled and adjusted his glasses.

Returning to the car (a stunning 1965 Mercury Comet) after the movie, Lois again was surprised—this time by a waiting Thermos container of ice cream. You guessed it. It was pralines and cream.

"What a super man," Lois sighed.

Does Clark have super powers? Maybe, but he also could have secretly placed the gift in the popcorn while he was in the lobby and could have arranged for a buddy, contacted from a lobby phone booth, to place the appropriate type of ice cream in the car.

62

—Rhett and Scarlett were involved in a tempestuous affair when Scarlett decided to take charge of her romance. One evening she picked Rhett up and headed for the local drive-in. This Southern "gentleman" was intrigued to find the car filled with an abundance of fringy and fluffy pillows. (It's absolutely amazing what Scarlett can do with old drapes.)

After paying for both of them, our heroine nudged her car into a parking space and then motioned for Rhett to remain silent. Scarlett reached behind her seat and produced a basket filled with Southern-fried zucchini and mushrooms. This was followed by an eleven-course picnic dinner.

When the movie ended, Rhett lunged for Scarlett. She cooled his ardor by whacking his romance with a buggy whip.

"Frankly, Scarlett . . ." Rhett pleaded, "I aim to make you mine."

"Well, Rhett," Scarlett whispered starting the car, "tomorrow is another day."

—And Han and Leia had a hot romance that was, unfortunately, marred by a number of less-than-warming interruptions. For example, on their way to the movies one Friday night, Han remembered some very important papers that had to be picked up at the office. Leia understood. Things were like that in Han's import-export business.

Entering the darkened office, Han took Leia's hand and led her to the conference room. Instead of turning on the lights, he flicked his Bic and lit a candle. In the flickering romantic glow Leia saw a waiting bottle of champagne with an assortment of un-earthly delights (compliments of Sara Lee).

They cuddled on pillows placed on the plushly carpeted floor and, through the magic of a rented videotape recorder and large screen TV, settled in to watch their favorite movie—*Return of the Jump-Starters*.

Leia snuggled close to Han and whispered, "I love you." "I know," he replied.

And for some jump-starters, movies, dinners, and the like are just not exciting enough. They crave action. They need to know, like "Wild Woman of Baltimore" . . .

Q. What can I do that's really crazy and really romantic?

A. Lots. Really.

—Terry found an original way to make his first date with Kay a memorable one. Here's how she tells the story:

"I had only known Terry a short time when he asked me out for 'lunch' on a Saturday afternoon. It surprised me when we drove a little distance outside of town, but I didn't think anything too unusual was up. We drove until we got to a museum complex about twelve miles away. There, Terry stopped the car, opened the door for me, and gave me a little daypack to wear.

"Believe it or not, I still didn't think anything different was going on. We breezed through the gates and headed immediately for an artificial cave exhibit at the museum. Once there, Terry reached into his pack and pulled out two signs that said, 'One Moment Please. Men Working.' He then put one sign at the entrance of the cave, waited for the people in the exhibit to leave, and then placed the other sign at the exit.

"In the rest of his pack was a bouquet of flowers and a linen tablecloth. In my pack he had hidden a complete picnic lunch. We sat, all alone, in the middle of this beautiful cave and ate and talked for what seemed like hours. No one discovered our private picnic. But, that 'danger' of discovery just made it more fun."

—Kim enjoyed a little daring romance at a party held by a friend. "This guy's always been known for being different," she wrote, "so I wasn't too surprised when I got an invitation to an 'Upstairs Party.' It wasn't until I got there that I found out that 'upstairs' was on the roof of a seven-floor building.

"Before I knew it, I had climbed the stairs to the roof and was dancing, yes, dancing on top of this building. He had even hired a band to play up there."

—Anne dared to be different and found it to be an elevating experience. "I wanted to do something unique to surprise my fiance. So, one night when he was working late at his office, I came by to 'keep him company.' On the way down to the garage afterwards, I pushed the 'Stop' button on the elevator and pulled a small bottle of champagne from my purse. Boy, was he surprised! And, boy, did he like it."

—Geri wanted to give her romance a lift so she set up a "daring" hot air balloon ride. "It was something he said he would like to do 'sometime,' so I surprised him with an hour-and-a-half flight. It truly was a romantic treat for both of us. The feeling of floating was unbelievable and when we landed in a family's backyard twenty-five miles from where we took off, it was a treat for them also."

Where do you find a hot air balloon to rent? You can either shoot one down or you can check in your phone book (honestly) under the heading "Balloons-Manned."

—And more down-to-earth but adventuresome jump-starters can enjoy the thrill of a cross-country ski trip. Here's a tip from Linda, a longtime ski touring fan: "Ladies, try this. At some point during your trip, stop with your loved one for a breather . . . and then strip. Not all the way, of course. Wear a bikini under your cold-weather gear. It's amazing how your partner will invariably offer to help keep you warm."

4

"I'd Really Like to Get to Know My Latest Girlfriend and I Mean Know Her (Catch My Drift?). Got a Sure-Fire Quick-Action Plan?"

No. And it's "slam-bam-you-clean-up-the-mess-ma'm" guys like you who give romance a bad name.

Maybe you should know what romance *isn't*.

—Romance *isn't* scoring with your date, lighting up a cigarette, and then saying, "Hey, baby. My name's Rock. What's yours?"

—Romance *isn't* 413½ notches on the corner post of your waterbed.

—Romance *isn't* lifetime subscriptions to every men's magazine including *Vinyl Monthly*.

—Romance *isn't* saying "Don't worry, honey. I'll call you," and then trashing her phone number as soon as you get out the door.

—Romance *isn't* declaring you know "How to Make Love to a Woman" as though she were a production model Buick.

—Romance *isn't* "Hey, baby. What's your sign?" extra-strength mouthwash, and the oil from a thousand musks.

—Romance *isn't* making a date and then standing her up

for something "better"—like the National Wrist-Wrestling Finals on TV.

—Romance *isn't* showing up dirty and unshaven just because it "makes me look even more macho."

—Romance *isn't* complaining to your lover, "But Zelda, Yvonne, Darleen, Regina, Helga, Anastasia, Maude, and all the other girls liked it that way."

Real men don't eat quiche because they don't know how to pronounce it. And real men don't know romance because they don't know where to find it . . .

Q. I'm a macho man who's looking for romance. What do you think about singles bars?—"Batting 1000"

A. I think singles bars are great if you want to stay that way. Why? Because almost everything in the bar scene works against discovering real romance. (Your batting average, for instance.)

Here are just a few more examples of what I mean:

—Relationships begin with communication. It's tough to chat with "The Plasmatics" dying in the background.

—Alcohol in quantity is about as romantic as a week-long case of food poisoning. You can't be "wonderful" or "sexy" if you can no longer pronounce them.

—Regulars at singles bars are not known for their subtlety. I think events like "Drink and Drown Night" or "Midget Mud Wrestling" say it all.

—Singles bars are the last bastion of the cigarette smoking scene. This probably explains why these places frequently smell like smoldering camels.

—And singles bars use a time-clock approach: Punch in at 9:00. Score at 11:00. Punch out at 11:03. It may be as reliable as a Timex, but John Cameron Swazey would not be amused.

So, how does a real man find romance? He can start by learning the word, "hello" . . .

Q. I read where you said the best opening line is "hello." Can't you be a little more original?—"Still Swinging Single"

A. Yes, I can be more original, but it certainly wouldn't be more effective. A good old-fashioned hello still leads the way as the world's best introduction.

Just for real men, however, here's a list of the world's *worst* opening lines. Use these babies at your own risk:

—Hi, baby. I'm gay. Can you help me?

—You know, sweetheart, you'd be real foxy if you lost about twelve pounds.

—Gee, I've never seen hair that color before.

—Darling, I don't know your name. Last night in my dreams all I could call you was beautiful.

—Wow, what's that perfume you're wearing? I knew I smelled something strange out in the parking lot.

—Want to come up to my place and listen to my "Electric Prunes" record collection?

—Remember me? I met you last year at Frank's party. I never forget a dress.

—You know, they can do wonders with face lifts these days.

—I can tell by the Ragu on your chin that you like Italian food.

—So, what's it like to be over forty?

—Want a breath mint?

—I hear some men really like women with big hips.

—Is it true that homely women are easy?
—How long have you been growing that moustache?
—I admire a woman who isn't afraid to be unfashionable.
—I see the diet craze hasn't gotten to you yet.
—Wow, you can really put down the booze.
—Where do you ever find pantyhose that big?
—How's the weather up there?
—Wasn't I once married to you?
—Let me tell you about Reverend Moon.
—I bet it's tough to find clothes to fit a figure like yours.
—Come here often? I live in the back.
—Damn. I thought you were my friend Bob.
—You know baby, you look a lot like my wife.

Fortunately, most guys aren't "real" men. The great majority appreciate affection and tenderness and will take "mushiness" over macho any day.

Where then, does the image of the "manly" man come from? No, not from Liberace. It comes from television. And movies . . .

Q. Please settle a bet. We'd like to know who you think the most manly television or movie star is. About half of us have picked Tom Selleck and the other half are split between Erik Estrada and Robert Wagner.—"On Coffee Break in Fort Wayne"

A. I'm sorry Tom, Erik, and Robert. My vote for the single most "manly" star goes to E.T. Sure, E.T.'s beer belly may hang a little close to the ground, but true "manliness" comes from the heart—and based on heart, E.T. is Mr. Universe.

I'm not the only one who believes manliness has little to do with muscles. Listen to these letters from women in love with *real* men.

—"I'd dated tons of guys," wrote JoAnne, "but none of them really impressed me. Several had fancy cars and others took me to very expensive places. Basically, they were all duds. Then I met John. I wasn't very impressed at first—he looks sort of like Radar from "M*A*S*H," but it didn't take me long to learn that this guy was sincere. When he said he cared for me, I knew it wasn't just another line. I'd rather have a nice guy who really cares than a gorgeous guy who lies through his shiny teeth."

—"I would like to nominate my partner, James, for the title of 'World's Greatest Romantic,'" wrote Lynn. "Sometimes I think he understands me better than I understand myself. If I'm sick, he knows it. If I'm depressed, even just a little bit, he knows it. And if I need a little moral support, he's always right there."

—And Marilyn wrote, "My partner is the best in the world. I've never been much of a cook and the cake I baked him for his birthday was a total disaster. One-half crumbled when I took it out of the pan and the frosting looked even worse. My wonderful man, however, treated it as though it were a masterpiece. Later he told me, 'I figure if you can love me with my wrinkled body, I can love a cake with a few wrinkles, too.'"

5

"There Is This Beautiful 'Mystery Lady' I've Been Trying to Meet. What Can I Do to Show Her I'm Amazing, Wonderful, and a Whole Lot of Fun?"

The best way to be amazing and wonderful is to be yourself (or to hire Robert Redford to do all your stunts). And the best way to be a whole lot of fun is to remember that, when it comes to romance and mystery ladies, *nothing* is impossible.

Your mission, should you decide to accept it, is to examine, follow, and enjoy this six-point jump-starting plan:

STEP ONE:

Before you can win one for your favorite gipper, you need to know the rules of the game. Fortunately, they're as easy to remember as R-O-M-A-N-C-E.

R—*Relax,* relax, relax. Despite what you may be thinking, romance, while extremely contagious, is rarely fatal. But, oh, what a way to go.

O—*Observe* and listen. There's a great old song that goes, "Find out what she likes and how she likes it and give it to her just that way." Does she like piña coladas? Does she like walks in the rain? Is she not into yoga . . . well, you get the idea. You'll be amazed what you can learn just by

73

observing and listening (and I mean legally, of course).

M—*Make* the time. The single most valuable thing you can give to anyone is time. Your mystery lady will remain just that if you only pitch your woo (wasn't he a Chinese reliever for the Yankees?) during a thirteen-minute coffee break.

A—*Attack.* Take the initiative. Unless she also sells vacuum cleaners, your intended is not going to come knock-knocking at your door. Determine your jump-starting strategy and *attack*—figuratively speaking, of course.

N—*Never* demand anything specific in return. You're not dealing in commodity futures here. You might get what you want and, then again, you might not. Take pleasure in showing your affection. And, if she continually ignores you, take pleasure in showing your affection—to someone else.

C—*Care* to be different. Do you have any idea how many boring schmucks she could have her choice of? Probably 117. Care to be *different* and show her you're one in a million (more or less).

E—*Enjoy* yourself. Can I let you in on a secret? You're a pain in the you-know-what when you're not having a good time. Keep telling yourself, "This is the fun part." Who knows? You might be right.

STEP TWO:

"All right, so how do I get her to notice me?" Well, you could always pin money to yourself. I hear that works real well. Or, you could be direct, assertive, and sneaky—all at the same time. Here are a few suggestions for getting her attention at work:

—Is she copying, collating, folding, binding, and stapling straight through lunch? Be a pal and bring her something from the deli or be a gourmand and send out for pizza. Don't

74

ask. Just do it.

—Back massages are standard fare for overworked shoulders. Why not take this one step further and, as Robert, a very popular executive suggested, offer a foot massage to your coworker in need? Be gentle, but firm.

—Everybody knows that a pile of "Urgent" messages, when left by themselves, will reproduce faster than a bunny named Xerox. Brighten your mystery lady's life by leaving just one more note that says, "Call me ASAP so I can tell you how wonderful you are."

—In the first chapter we discussed the meanings of different types of flowers. One good way to get her attention is to send her a bouquet of something a little unusual—like yellow roses—anonymously. Then, instead of saying, "Hey, how'd you like those buds I sent ya?" just put a single flower of the same variety in a small vase on *your* desk.

—And, if you'd like to arrange a lunch date but your schedules just don't seem to jibe, try this: Set up an "important" appointment in your office (or a borrowed one) for the next day right before noon. Then, when you're both safely inside, pull out a three-course picnic lunch. Tell whomever to "Hold all calls." After all, important partnership plans are being discussed.

STEP THREE:

Speaking of picnics, one sure way to be amazing and wonderful is to repeat your office performance with the real thing in the great outdoors.

Rich folk, like Redford, have it easy. When they go on a picnic they grab their butler, a six-pack of caviar, and confidently leap into the Rolls. When the rest of us go on a picnic, we grab our mutt, a handful of potato salad, and hope the car starts.

If you're a jump-starter on a budget, here are some hints:

—There are two different opinions about the food at a picnic. One side in this food fight believes that food is the *most* important element, while the other side believes it's the *least*. Personally, I think it's a waste of time to worry about the guacamole dip when you've got something more entertaining to nibble on.

If you've got a little money, have your favorite deli prepare a meat and cheese tray. If you don't, just pick out a selection of your luncheon favorites (anything but bologna), a variety pack of cheese, a loaf of real French bread (not the squishy type—that's reserved for romantics without teeth), and a bottle of chilled wine (avoid anything priced under $1.00).

—Once you've got the food, where do you put it? While some picnickers do a great imitation of a bag lady, a wicker basket is preferred. If you don't have a basket, take a sturdy, medium-sized box, stuff it with your goodies, and then gift wrap it.

—Now, what do you hold your picnic on? No, not "each other." A large tablecloth or blanket is preferred. (A king-sized air mattress isn't bad, either.)

STEP FOUR:

By now you're sure to have gotten the attention of your mystery lady. How do you keep it? You use plenty of jump-starting grease—aka "consistency." Check out the Jump-Starting Calendar in Chapter 3 for some stimulating ideas.

STEP FIVE:

In your quest to be amazing, wonderful, and a whole lot of fun, you've probably also read the latest thirty-seven manuals on thoroughly modern sex. If I could just add one piece of old-fashioned advice: Don't forget romance. Take the time to get to know each other. Take the time to really set the mood. Take the time to care.

STEP SIX:

And, if you'd *really* like to impress your now not-so-mysterious lady with your taste in people, ask her to marry you. Yes, I said marry—m-a-r-r-y. It beats going to bed with Johnny Carson for the rest of your life.

And for those of you who, unlike Johnny, are proposing for the *first* time, here are a few ideas:

—Richard realized he'd met the love of his life when he saw her creatively scooping ice cream at a local soda shop. After dating her for about a year, he decided it was time to pop the big one.

For that all-important evening, Richard rented a chauffeured limousine and whisked Sue, his intended, off to the fanciest restaurant in town. Dinner was superb, but the clincher was dessert. Instead of the flaming tableside dessert she had ordered, the waiter brought Sue a simple vanilla ice cream cone—with a diamond engagement ring encircling its bottom.

—Cliff's proposal to Joan also featured an after dinner treat. Just as they finished dessert, their waiter brought Joan an elegantly gift-wrapped box. When she opened it, a heart-shaped balloon on a string rose from its center. Attached to the string was, you guessed it, Joan's engagement ring. (By the way, this airborne approach is recommended for *inside* use only.)

—Tim and Jane had been planning to get married since their high school days. Knowing that she would get suspicious if he got too fancy, Tim invited Jane over for "dinner and little hot-tubbing." Nothing amazing happened during dinner, but after they'd been tubbing for just a few minutes he asked, "So, what do you think about marriage." Having heard this before, Jane answered, "Are you serious?" Knowing a cue when he saw one, Tim dove under the water and magically pulled out a diamond ring from the middle of the bubbles. (No, he didn't have a special arrangement with Jacques Cousteau. Before their date, Tim had hidden the ring in a rock-weighted baggie at the bottom of the tub.)

—Randy added a little magic of his own to his girlfriend's Valentine's Day gift. At the bottom of a hardly standard two-pound box of chocolates, he placed an engagement ring and written proposal of marriage. It wasn't until two days later that she found her surprise, called Randy, and said "yes." (It might be best to avoid this approach when proposing to rabid chocolate-aholics.)

—And Todd arranged a special evening that I was lucky enough to help with.

On a Monday, Todd invited his girlfriend, Denise, out for a fun-filled Saturday evening at a theater specializing in ragtime music and good old-fashioned melodrama. To heighten the excitement, he suggested that he would "have a surprise" for her then.

That Saturday arrived and Todd, dressed in his finest, picked up Denise, and took her to the show. When they got there, they were immediately ushered into the theater and taken to the best table in the house. Waiting on that table was a bouquet of one dozen long-stemmed red roses. It was at this point that Denise began to get a little suspicious.

Everything proceeded normally until the first intermission when a waitress appeared carrying a large, gift-wrapped box for—you guessed it—Denise. "Could a ring be hidden in there?" she wondered. Yes, it could be—but it wasn't. The box contained a love note and 67 Snickers bars (her favorite).

During the second intermission the piano-playing host announced that he had a special message for someone in the audience. Denise just sat there smiling until she heard, "Ladies and gentlemen, we at the theater would like to announce the engagement this evening of Todd and Denise."

Denise, her mouth wide open, looked at the piano player and then at Todd, who was holding—you guessed it again—the ring. Tears flowed down her cheeks as she cried "Yes!" and threw her arms around her new fiance. The crowd burst into applause.

"Wow, this is just like Miss America," a girl sitting next to me said. I'm sure Denise would agree.

Not all jump-starters are ready for marriage. Take this one, for instance . . .

Q. I'm thirteen years old and I'm in the eighth grade. There is this girl in English that always stares at me during class. My friend's teen-age sister told me that she probably likes me and that I should ask her out on a date. I want to, but how can I since I don't even know her?—"Curious"

A. Some people might say that at thirteen you're too young to think about dating. I'm not one of them. However, it's a good idea for jump-starters of all ages to think about making friends before taking a relationship any further.

Your friend's teen-age sister is right when she says that your bug-eyed classmate probably likes you. And you're right, too, when you say that you should get to know her before asking her out.

Here are a few suggestions to help you break the ice:

—Start by saying "hello." It's pretty tough to get to know someone if you don't talk to them. In a classroom you have all sorts of opportunities to strike up a conversation. Something like, "Isn't (name a teacher) a mega-nerd?" might be a perfect way to start.

—Don't ignore "mini-dates." While it might not be your favorite four-star restaurant, the school lunchroom is a good place to get acquainted. In fact, once you're there, conversation is easy. Start with something obvious like, "Isn't it amazing how the hamburger can crawl all by itself across the plate?" and hope she has a sense of humor.

—Concentrate on having fun, not on being perfect. On my very first "date" in junior high school, I took my girl bicycling and promptly rode into a tree. And it was her bike. Keep in mind that everybody makes mistakes. Some of us just make more than others.

For inexperienced—and experienced—jump-starters, here's a handy list of mistake-preventing *do's* and *don'ts:*

1) *Do* make a plan for your date before you ask her out. Remember to find out times, places, cost, transportation, movie titles, etc.

Don't just wing it. The worst advice I ever got as a neophyte romantic was to tell my date that we'd "have a blast" but that I didn't know exactly what we'd do. She suggested that I should call her when I knew, but preferably "sometime next year."

2) *Do* formally ask your date out. If you feel a little weird asking her face-to-face, the telephone has been known to work, too.

Don't say, "Why don't we go out sometime," and then expect her to be ready whenever you call. Your older brother may do this, but if you'd like to live to see fourteen, don't.

3) *Do* dress well. You don't have to wear a tux, but clean clothes, at least, are a must. And let your date know ahead of

time how fancy the evening, or afternoon, is apt to be so she can dress accordingly.

Don't ask her out for an elegant evening and then show up in your best grungy T-shirt and dress sneakers.

4) *Do* take the time to meet her parents when you pick up your date. You don't have to tell them your life story, a simple "Hello, Mr. and Mrs. Slobotnik, I'm _____" will do.

Don't pull up to her house, or have your ride pull up, and then sit in the car and honk the horn. This is no time for the mating call of the wild Chevette.

5) *Do* open the door for your date at every appropriate opportunity—leaving her home, getting in and out of the car, at the restaurant, theater, concert, etc.

Don't walk into a restaurant first and then let the door slam into her face. This is a guaranteed way to break her heart—as well as her nose.

6) *Do* select a restaurant with her feelings in mind. While you might just love "Frank's Pickles Au Gratin," try picking a place that has general appeal.

Don't force her to eat seriously messy food on your first date. Burgers are a good choice. Finger-lickin' ribs are not.

7) And *do* take the time to thank your date, even if you had a less-than-awesome time.

Don't ignore her or, worse yet, demand a good night kiss (or more). Relax and let things take their own course. Before you think I'm suggesting this because of your age, realize that this is the rule I follow on my first dates.

Even with the best set of rules, foul-ups will occasionally happen. But, what if—like "Columbus Klutz"—you still seem to be a mistake magnet no matter how hard you try? . . .

Q. I feel like such a jerk. Last night I went out on a date with a girl from work and dropped a plate of spaghetti in my lap—and I'm thirty-four years old. Am I cursed? Who would ever want to be with me?

A. Don't worry. One lost load of pasta does not a klutz make. In fact, some people even find a little clumsiness cute.

To help you know when you've gone from cute to klutz, watch out for these danger signals:

"You know you're a romantic klutz when . . ."

—On your return trip to an intimate restaurant they only set your table with spoons.

—You go to the store to buy candles for a midnight bubble bath and the clerk recommends a waterproof flashlight.

—Every time you buy champagne at your neighborhood liquor store, they throw in a free bath towel and a pair of safety goggles.

—Your friends christen your new king-sized waterbed "The Titanic."

—Your local formal wear store will only rent you a rubberized tuxedo.

—You invite your date out for an afternoon drive and she shows up in flame-retardant hockey gear.

—The most exciting thing you've caused by necking is traction.

—The theater concession stand will only sell you popcorn one kernel at a time.

—Your swimming trip to the beach is picketed by the "Save the Whales" Foundation.

—On a Saturday outing to the country your first-aid kit is better stocked than your picnic basket.

—Ben-Gay is your idea of an erotic massage lotion.

—You ask a forest ranger where a good place for boating

is and he recommends the YMCA.

—You go to buy a diamond for your partner and the clerk tries to sell you something "less breakable."

—You go on a brief moonlight walk and your date brings along a flare gun and survival gear.

—You ask the band to play your song and they strike up "Nearer My God to Thee."

—Your loved one refuses to sit on a porch swing with you without a net.

—Your bicycle-built-for-two comes with air bags.

—Your romantic ski trip is banned by the "Society for the Prevention of Cruelty to Trees."

—Your get-away trip to Mexico is filmed for an American Tourister luggage commercial.

—The pharmacist throws in a free box of baby supplies whenever you buy contraceptives.

Fortunately, even the most klutzy of episodes can be banished from memory by love (or through professional hypnosis). While a simple "I love you" is always appropriate, you may be looking for something a little different . . .

Q. At last I've found a woman I love. My problem is that I'd like to tell her in a truly special way. Any ideas?—"Three Little Wordless"

A. If "I love you" seems too domestic, it's definitely time to enter the world of foreign affairs. Here's a list of how to say "I love you" in the languages of a number of exotic countries.

—Africa	"Nakupenda"
—Brazil	"Te amo"
—China	"Wo ai nei"
—Eskimo	"Nagligivaget"
—France	"Je t'aime"

—Germany	"Ich liebe dich"
—Greece	"S'agapo"
—Hawaii	"Aloha wau ia oe"
—India	"Mai tumhe pyar karta hu"
—Ireland	"Thaim in grabh leat"
—Israel	"Ani ohev otakh"
—Italy	"Ti amo"
—Japan	"Anata ga suki desu"
—Mexico	"Te quiero"
—Neanderthal	"Ugh, ugh—baby"
—Netherlands	"Ik houd van jou"
—Paraguay	"Rho hi hu"
—Russia	"Ya lyublyu tyebya"
—Saudi Arabia	" 'Uhibbuki"
—Spain	"Te amo"
—Sweden	"Jag alskar dig"
—United Kingdom	"You make lovely tea."
—United States	"Jump-start me"

6

"Am I the Only One Who's Single? How Does an Unattached Woman Find Romance?"

If life were like television, finding romance would be as easy as buying the latest breath freshener and bumping into the nearest man. In reality, finding romance is about as easy as bumping into the nearest wall—repeatedly.

How can you jump-start your love life without flattening your face? You can start by considering these guidelines for F-I-N-D-I-N-G romance:

F—*Forget* everything you've seen about romance on the soaps, in commercials, or at the movies. Real-life romance is not like that. It's better—*you* are the star.

I—*Ignore* excuses. Make a list of all the good, true, and rational reasons you have for not getting your romantic butt into gear. Then burn it.

N—*Never* say never. Romance can happen at any time, at any place, and at *any age*. How do I know? I've received hundreds of letters from the experts—real people who have found romance. (And if you don't believe that mature romantics can find love and tenderness, I know a number of senior citizens who strongly disagree and would be happy to beat you to a pulp.)

D—*Don't* throw in the towel. If you think I'm repeating myself, you're right. Remember, love at first sight is still alive and well, but sometimes it can take years.

I—*Introductions* are not necessary. The best way to jump-start Mr. Right (or Mr. Let Me at Least Give You a Test-Drive) is to go straight to the source. Don't wait for a friend to introduce you—this is one sure way to short-circuit a connection.

N—*Nuke* your television. What's the greatest threat to finding romance? No, it's not terminal dandruff, mountain-sized panty lines, or fuming fungus breath. It's your TV. Unplug it now. Don't worry. You can turn on more than a Sony.

G—*Get Out!* One single woman wrote that she would sit at home and order pizza every night just so she could meet the delivery boys; 1,117 pepperonis and 16 pounds later, she decided to quit wasting her time on anchovies and to get out and start fishing for the real thing.

But, what if you've been fishing for a long time and haven't gotten so much as a nibble? Before we talk about changing bait, let's first consider the catch itself.

THE "I DON'T EVEN KNOW IF ROMANCE IS WORTH IT SO WHY GO THROUGH ALL THIS HASSLE?" QUIZ

Here's a list of a number of things that many women consider their "keys to happiness" (and no, Tom Selleck isn't one of them). Your first step in this quiz is to pick the two (and only two) things that are the most important to you:

—Money

—Fame

—Power

—Love

—Sex

—Chocolate

—A Gold American Express Card

(Just for the sake of argument, let's assume that if you have money, fame, power, and love you can have all the sex, chocolate, and Gold American Express Cards you want.)

Now that you've picked your top two keys to happiness—and I'm willing to wager that they're money and love—the next step is to pick just one of these two. (To make things interesting, if you pick money you'll never know love, and if you pick love, you'll never be rich.) Which will it be?

Time's up. Love wins. (I'm a sucker for a happy ending.)

For almost everyone, love is the key, the tops, the big enchilada. Now, which type of love do you want? Do you want attentive love or inattentive love? Attentive love is where you ask your Monday Night Football watching honey if he loves you, and he replies, "More than the world, darling. In fact, let me turn off this silly old game and take you dancing." Inattentive love is where you do the same thing and your pigskin partner replies, "(Burp) Yo, woman, fetch me a beer."

Unless you're really into pain, you've picked the first example—attentive love. Now, what is this attention that makes love work called? What is the name for this ultimate key to happiness? It's romance. And it's worth it. End of quiz.

Enough with rules and tests. It's time for action . . .

Q. I love romance, but I just don't know if I'm up to it—physically, I mean. What can I do?—"Bo Derek, I'm Not"

A. So what if you're not built like Bo. Most guys aren't made like Tarzan, either. (Cheeta—maybe.)

The key is to be the best you can be—or at least a rough imitation of it. Here's just a quickie list of tips:

Diet. Frankly, I don't know how anyone can feel good about her body when she's continually trying to annihilate parts of it. Jump-start your bod through *exercise*—and limit your hot-fudge banana extravaganzas to just twice a week.

Dress. Be comfortable. How attractive will you be if your six-inch heels give you nosebleeds? Be smart, be classy, and think comfort. (And don't wear skin-tight jeans if you're planning to pig-out on pasta.)

Hair. Definitely.

Cleanliness. Always.

And *Perfume.* Think of perfume not as a powerful appetizer, but as a delicate dessert—one that must be gently nibbled to be fully appreciated. (In other words, avoid any brand marked "Heavy Duty.")

Now that you're in fine physical form, it's time to consider . . .

Q. Where can I go and what can I do to find romance?

A. How many times have you heard the suggestions, "Join a singles' group," "Do volunteer work," "Get active in your church," or "Move to an all-male mining community in Zanzibar"? While these aren't bad suggestions, you've probably already thought of them.

The secret to successful jump-starting is to make a plan of things that you *like* to do. It makes absolutely zilch sense to spend 150 bucks a month on a health club if you detest sweat. And it's less-than-worthless to do volunteer work if your idea of charity is writing a $3.00 check to the "Save the

Mercedes Fund.''

All you need to do is this: Get out a pen and a piece of paper and write down at least seven things that you like to do (sleeping, snoozing, and snoring don't count). Then, turn your list into a schedule and stick to it. Take things easy at first. You're shooting for exposure, not exhaustion. Here's one woman's plan:

Monday—''I like to swim.'' On Monday evening she puts on her suit and does laps (about four—very slowly) at the YMCA. (Yes, I said the YMCA. She's no dummy.) It costs a whole lot less than a health club and there's no competition from Playboy Bunny clones.

Tuesday—''I like to eat.'' Every Tuesday she dines at a different restaurant—alone. This way she enjoys a continually changing variety of food, saves money on weekday specials, and attracts like-minded male diners.

Wednesday—''I like animals.'' No, this is not the night she dates the Dallas Cowboys football team. Wednesday is when she takes her dog to obedience training at the park. Frankly, she admits that she hasn't met very many eligible men there, but she ''did get to pet an amazing Irish Wolfhound.''

Thursday—''I like movies.'' No, not the kind where flexible adolescents perform illicit acts in front of E.T. On Thursday she's a member of the ''Classic Films Series'' sponsored by the local university. (Series of these kinds are popular throughout the country.) ''With the discussion sessions afterwards, this is a great way to meet people,'' she says.

Friday—''I like me.'' Each Friday night, unless she has a date, she prepares a candlelit dinner for one. Afterwards, she pours herself a snifter (or two) of brandy and reads a good book. ''I especially liked the *Buns* book,'' she reveals.

Saturday—"I like bicycling." Weather permitting, she packs her bike in her car and heads for a nearby regional park. Why the park? "There's no traffic, the scenery is nicer, and the guys are cuter," she answers.

Sunday—"I like to travel." About every other Sunday she packs up and heads out of town. A regular trip is a two-hour drive to "the area's best Mexican restaurant." On occasion, she'll even take a quickie flight to the "big city." "It might be a little expensive," she admits, "but, damn it, I'm worth it."

Here are a few more activities single jump-starters may want to consider:

WINTER

—Ice skating
—Skiing
—Sledding
—Hitting unsuspecting strangers with snowballs
—Building anatomically correct snow people
—Snowmobiling
—Hunting for a Christmas tree
—Shopping
—Drinking Irish Coffee
—Drinking Irish Coffee and then shopping
—Helping out with the holiday food drive

SPRING

—Picnicking
—Joining the "Let's Sit and Rest a Bit" hiking club
—Flying a kite
—Shopping
—Drinking Piña Coladas
—Drinking Piña Coladas and then shopping

90

—Tending a garden
—Preparing for a marathon (buy a new pair of sneakers)
—Helping out with your Neighborhood Watch program

SUMMER

—Snoozing by the pool
—Playing "We Wouldn't Know a Bat If It Hit Us" scratch league softball
—Making hand-cranked ice cream
—Illegally transporting fireworks for a Fourth of July festival
—Sitting out on your balcony or porch in the evening (Ignore anyone yelling, "Stella!")
—Catching a new summer release at a weekend movie matinee
—Going to concerts and plays in the park
—Shopping
—Drinking Strawberry Margaritas
—Drinking Strawberry Margaritas and then shopping
—Taking flowers to a friend
—Sailing (or riding your bike through a sprinkler)
—Skinny dipping ("But officer, my bathing suit must be around here somewhere. By the way, do you know what broad shoulders you have?")
—Volunteering at your local crisis nursery

FALL

—Watching a high school football game
—Jumping into a pile of leaves (this is not recommended for heavy users of hair spray)
—Helping out with a friend's orchard harvest (or treating a buddy to a McDonald's hot apple pie)
—Taking a hot air balloon ride

—Winning third place in a seriously strange Halloween costume contest

—Shopping . . . (Improvise on the rest)

—Doing something crazy, like watching a Marx Brothers Film Festival

—Doing something even crazier, like being a volunteer in a political campaign

So far, a little decent exposure has been the goal of this jump-starting campaign. Now, it's time to go even further . . .

Q. There's a guy that I'd like to get to know better, but I don't know how to go about it. His name is Robert and he's a teller at a bank. What would be a good way of getting to know him without being too forward? I'm really desperate because I've been seeing him at this bank for over a year.— "Desperate for Help in Fort Lauderdale"

A. Breaking the ice can be extremely difficult, especially if it's grown into a glacier. Fortunately, nothing fractures frigidity faster than a steady romantic flame. Try this ten-point heart-warming plan:

1) If you're stuck for words—and even if you're not—try an ice-breaking smile. Love, war, and you-know-what, has been known to be jump-started by a well-timed grin.

2) Say, "Hello Robert." This is more than just a greeting. (If you don't believe me, think about this: Remember in high school when a girl friend would come running up and say, "Guess what? Tommy loves me." And you'd ask how she knew, and she'd say, "I just know. Tommy loves me." And you'd ask what he did, and she'd say "Nothing. But he *loves* me." And you'd nearly wring her neck and demand to know exactly how she knew and she'd say, "Because, Tommy said . . . hello.")

3) Go ahead and give him a compliment. There's no doubt that you feel he's just a tad more attractive than the Hunchback of Notre Dame. Tell him what beautiful eyes he has. After that, he'll probably like you for more than just your money.

4) If words fail you, go straight for his stomach. There are few men alive today who cannot be enticed by a shapely chocolate chip cookie.

5) Give him a flower. Try pinning a single rosebud to your jacket and then taking it off (the rose, not the jacket) and pinning it on his. This approach may not win awards for subtlety but it works.

6) Take him a good book. Make sure it shows him how intelligent, discriminating, and fun you are. Like this book, for example.

7) When he does something nice for you—like counting up all your loose change and making it into those little coin sausages—send him a little thank you note. You don't have to write chapters, just a short "Thank you for all your help, handsome" is perfect.

8) If you know when his birthday is, go ahead and send him a card. (If you find out when his anniversary is, go ahead and mail him a bomb.) Anything, no matter how inexpensive, is sure to get your message across.

9) Feel free to ask *him* out. I asked one hundred men if they would like it if a woman asked them out. Their answer? Every one of them said, "Yes!" and many of them wanted to know where they could find such a woman.

10) Keep on trying. If you don't seem to score with your bank teller immediately, just remember that interest compounds daily.

Everyone has an MDR, a "Minimum Daily Requirement of Romance," that must be filled every day. This romance can come not just from male-female relationships, but also from any caring relationship—friend to friend, sibling to sibling, parent to child, and the list goes on . . .

Q. I'm a single mother and I'd be interested in any suggestions you can offer on how to put romance into my relationship with my kids.—"Love My Children"

A. Especially when it comes to kindness and affection, children learn what they live. You can give your children a head start on happiness by showing them the importance of a lot of love and a little romance. For example:

—Pat shows her children how she feels in a wonderfully gentle way. "One weekend I accompanied my kids (ages six and eight) on a children's group hike sponsored by our church," she wrote. "When we arrived at our campsite that evening, an amazing thing happened. One of the counselors had the children, still bouncing around from the hike, sit around the campfire. Then, she went around to each of them and gently rubbed their shoulders, hands, and feet. Within minutes, these screaming kids had become quiet—even serene. I've found that this method works great on my kids at home and it lets me show them, directly, that I care."

—A number of parents have written that they add a little romance to their children's lives by writing them notes of encouragement and affection. They suggest that the notes can be placed in a lunchbox (or written on a lunch bag), hidden in a pants pocket or taped to a bicycle or video game. It's amazing how much a simple, "I think you're *awesome*," can mean to a child.

—John wrote that romance, especially with children, can be contagious. "Recently, a friend of mine went shopping with her two young boys and gave them a dollar for a couple of Cokes. They hurried down the mall and reappeared fifteen minutes later not with drinks, but with a tiny ceramic frog bought from one of the gift shops for their mother. When she asked why they had spent the money on her, they replied, 'Because you're always doing nice stuff for us.'"

—One mother I know shows her children she cares by throwing impromptu family pajama parties. "The pillow fights might get the den a little messy," she admitted, "but it's worth it."

—One of my all-time favorite romantic stories is this one from Cindy. "I wanted to share with you a romantic thing my seven-year-old daughter did for me," she wrote. "I asked her to make my bed one morning because I was running late. She did, and added a wonderful romantic touch: a red silk rose on my pillow. It was such a nice gesture. I have since placed the rose on *her* pillow when I've made her bed."

—If you're looking for a fun way to brighten up your child's life, why not place a personal note in the classified ad section of your newspaper? Congratulations for a good report card, a mega-amazing game of Donkey Kong, or a little extra household effort are always in order.

—And Marnie suggests this for older children: "When my children were younger, I used to play in puddles with them and then blame the mess on 'splashes from cars' if anyone over the age of five asked why we were so dirty," she said. "Now that they're grown, when they visit I do my best to remember the little things that they like—one of my sons is a raisin bread fiend, for example. It's these little things that really show you care."

There are some little things that show you *don't* care, too. "Still Waiting in Lakewood, Colorado" found this out and she wrote . . .

Q. Being the hopeless young romantic that I am, I am confused as to why I am frequently stood up by the men who ask me out. It doesn't happen every time, but more times than I care to admit I have been left hanging. Do you have any advice?

A. There is a name for men who habitually stand up their dates—jerks. And while there's nothing you can do about these guys, except ignore them, here are three things you can do to cut down on other dating disasters.

—Don't be afraid to ask for specifics. If the guy isn't together enough to know when, where, and what he's asking you to do, tell him to spend the evening with someone he really loves—himself.

—On first dates, arrange to meet at a neutral place, like a restaurant. As a good female friend of mine explained, "I never meet guys for first dates at bars or have them pick me up at my house. I think it's best to meet in a nice restaurant. That way, if he stands you up you're not stuck in some dive. Or if he turns out to be a real weirdo, you still get a good meal and then don't have to worry about 'Bela Lugosi' following you home."

—And, get his telephone number. If he's got yours, it's only fair, right? One woman wrote that she went so far as to take her date's number and Visa card as "collateral" when he asked her out for a second date after standing her up the first time. "To tell you the truth," she said, "I was a little disappointed when he did show up. I had my heart set on this nice new watch."

Sometimes dates do more than just show up and this can create big problems, as "Teen Party Girl" discovered . . .

Q. I am a teen-age girl who loves to go to dances. But

96

every time a guy asks me to slow dance, he gets closer than close. A friend told me that when a guy asks you to slow dance, he only wants to let his hands wander, if you know what I mean. What should I do? How do you hint to guys to back off without them thinking you're weird?

A. Forget the hints. When a guy is suffering from wander lust, just tell him one word—"No!" (Sometimes you have to say it with your knee for him to get the message.) No matter what he, or anybody else says, a slow dance is no excuse for a hormonal wrestling match.

A physical relationship, even in today's "Hi, my name's Bob. Was it good for you, too?" world, should be an expression of caring and affection. Saying no is not weird, it's smart. Listen to what these very intelligent women have to say on the subject:

—"I had my first sexual experience when I was only sixteen," wrote Judy. "It took me a lot of years and a lot of pain to learn that sex is not just a way to spend an evening— it's a way to express love. A physical relationship without love is empty. Now that I have a loving relationship, I can really see the difference."

—Paula also believes that love is vital. "In college, I thought that the way to be popular was to 'date' as many guys as possible," she said. "I was popular all right, but with all the wrong guys. Now, I'm looking for someone who cares. So what if I'm not the most popular anymore? I'm ready to wait for what's right."

—Lisa, too, looks for more than an evening of fast action. "After too many 'hot' relationships, I'm looking for some-one different. Someone who likes to hold hands . . . sit and gaze into each other's eyes . . . watch the moon come up. A guy who likes to share and give and does not like to use or be used. I'm looking for someone who likes me for me, not for what I'm willing to 'put out.'"

—"No matter what everybody seems to think, a kiss is not just a kiss," wrote Bobbi. "When I kiss a man it's because I care for him. And if he doesn't care for me, he can go smooch with himself."

—And Vanessa believes that it's okay to be "old-fashioned." She wrote: "The guys I used to go out with were like octopuses in heat. They had so many hands I never knew where they'd grab me next. I thought that all guys were that way—until I met my husband. We dated for over a year before we got married and the first time we went to bed together was on our wedding night. With other guys I had sex. Now I make love. I think that about says it all."

There you have it. The secret to jump-starting any relationship is to use a lot of love and a little romance. Is romance dead? Here's a question that I wish I'd received . . .

Q. I am twenty-nine years old. Some of my girlfriends say there is no such thing as romance. My sister says, "If you see it in a book, it's so." Please tell me the truth: Is there still romance?—"Virginia O., New York"

A. Virginia, your girlfriends are wrong. They have been affected by the problems of a difficult age. They cling to the "Me" generation when romance begins with "We."

All people, Virginia, need romance. From the most modern woman to the most macho man, we yearn to know that someone cares and we burn to know that we are loved.

And for each of us, romance is alive and real and just waiting to be jump-started. It doesn't take a truckload of money and it doesn't require a magical combination of deodorants. The key to finding romance is desire—a desire for something more, a desire for love and life the way they can be.

No romance! Thank love it exists. Indeed, as long as human hearts continue to beat, a secret smile, a single flower, and a gentle touch will continue to make glad the lives of lovers.